NATE NASRALLA

THAT SEEMS STRANGE

*finding a fulfilling life through
God's counterintuitive designs*

THAT SEEMS STRANGE

Copyright © 2020 by Live Forward Publishing, LLC and Nate Nasralla. All rights reserved. Printed in the United States of America. No part of this book may be used or reproduced in any manner whatsoever without written permission except in the case of quotations embedded in critical reviews, blogs, or articles.

For more information, email nate@natenasralla.com.
Subscribe and read more stories at www.natenasralla.com.

CONTENTS

Stories We Can't Predict   9
What this book is all about.

Time to Get Weird   13
Our quirks make us relatable.

Trespassing for the View   19
No plan is the best plan.

The Path to the Top   27
Lift others up and you'll end up on top.

My Life in a Duffel Bag   37
This life is just preparation for another.

The Time I Almost Went to Court   45
We can be right and wrong at the same time.

Living Life in a Tunnel   57
The more we give the more we gain.

Crying While Flying   65
Considering death creates a better life.

Feelings Are Like Honey   71
The most powerful sentences contain the fewest words.

CONTENTS

The Best Noodles I Ever Ate   81
Small choices can bring big consequences.

Gas Station Milkshakes   89
We never catch the things we chase.

How to Fly a Hot Air Balloon   95
We only see light on our darkest days.

Climbing Gray's in a Whiteout   105
Difficult experiences are the hardest to forget.

A Blind Haircut   115
We learn more with less information.

Sorry, Not This Year   123
Bring out the best in others to reveal the best in you.

A Rapping Flight Attendant   131
The simple things command the loudest praise.

Lock the Doors   137
Small inconveniences create big frustrations.

Overalls on an Airplane   147
The more we consume the less satisfied we feel.

The Start of a Stranger You   157

To E.

Life with you gets better and better every year.

stories we can't predict

God writes stories we could never predict. Ever since the beginning of time, he's been installing counterintuitive systems and unexpected realities into the fabric of our world. His methods cut against all our world's self-help books, seminars, and the conventional wisdom on how to live a fulfilling life. He even said to us, "My thoughts are nothing like your thoughts… my ways are far beyond anything you could imagine." (Isaiah 55:8)

God moves in unexpected ways over, and over, and over again all throughout the Bible. For example, one day a shepherd named Moses was walking through his pasture and noticed a bush that was lit on fire but not burning up. He said to himself, "I will go over and see this strange sight…" (Exodus 3:3) When he approached the bush, he found it was God calling him to lead his people out of slavery and away from Egypt. A bush on fire but not burning up is odd, to be sure, but what's truly striking is the fact God chose to use Moses to lead his people. Moses had spent the 40 years prior to this moment watching over sheep, yet God picks him to be the liberator of an entire nation. What kind of god picks an inarticulate, grimy field laborer to play the lead role in his story?

Later, God's son Jesus comes to earth and continues this trend. He picked a group of disciples to follow him and at first, they were thrilled. They left their jobs immediately, believing Jesus was planning to overthrow the Roman empire. They didn't want to miss their chance to make history. People measured power by military force during that age, but Jesus did what no military commander would ever consider. He rode a donkey, not a stallion. He washed feet. He paid his taxes on time. Ultimately, he died a gruesome and horrible death at the hands of the Romans – the very regime he was supposed to topple. Author A.W. Tozer describes this when he writes:

> *If man had his way, the plan of redemption would be an endless and bloody conflict. In reality, salvation was bought not by Jesus' fist, but by His nail-pierced hands; not by muscle but by love; not by vengeance but by forgiveness; not by force but by sacrifice. Jesus Christ our Lord surrendered in order that He might win; He destroyed His enemies by dying for them and conquered death by allowing death to conquer Him.*

The way in which Jesus overcame his enemies was not at all what his disciples anticipated. Can you imagine how they must have felt as they watched their supposed savior submit himself to humiliation and death? That wasn't how it was supposed to work! This wasn't the first or the only time Jesus surprised them, however. He was constantly correcting their assumptions, making comments like, "You have heard it said… but I say to you…"

Those who spread Jesus' message after his life did the same. In his letter to the Corinthian church, Paul said Jesus's crucifixion sounds like "foolishness" to most people. It upheaved convention and subverted human wisdom. (1 Corinthians 1:18-30) Paul also encouraged the church in Philippi to live, "[I]nnocent lives as children of God, shining like bright lights in a world full of crooked and perverse people." (Philippians 2:15)

Christians, according to Paul, should be different. They should stick out, just like the Christ they follow.

If we accept this call to swim upstream, we'll likely wonder if it's worth it. While God's stories always end with greater joy, goodness, and meaning, in the moment, his ways of working can seem strange. Bewildering, even. In fact, God often leads us through seasons we'd never choose if it were up to us. Seasons like grief, heartache, failure, depression, and loneliness. In the thick of them, we may question if there's any reason behind them. And when life feels backward and we ask God if we're *really* on the right track, it's easy to feel we're not getting any answers. Why doesn't he just respond in plain, audible English?

Our culture is quick to offer advice. The conventional wisdom on how to deal with these experiences usually sounds like, "Hustle harder. Buy more stuff. Follow your passion. Do what makes you happy." But if we take Jesus at his word when he says, "I have come that they may have life, and have it to the full," we'll discover that his directions for living a fulfilling life are often empty of our culture's norms. (John 10:10) Sometimes, we need to stop striving, give more, and elevate others' needs over our own.

Truth is, we often miss what God is trying to tell us because we expect his infinite nature to fit within the tiny aperture of our human perspective. But when we release the presumption our creator should work in ways straightforward to his creation, and we embrace his seemingly strange designs, we can begin to see the deeply meaningful plan he's been weaving together all along.

That's exactly why I wrote this book. I want you to see that as God fills your life with events and experiences that seem strange, he's ultimately working for both his glory and your good. And as you live aligned with his unexpected designs – not because you're "commanded" to, but because you crave the delight and true fulfillment it brings – my hope is that others who have no relationship with God will wonder, "Why are they so strange?" and ask you for the reason.

Before we continue, I'd like to provide two more points of context. Perhaps you don't actually believe in God. Maybe a "religious" friend gave you this book. If that's the case, I encourage you to read on. Each chapter has a mix of stories and lessons alongside biblical references. I think you'll find something to take away and apply to your life regardless of your religion.

On the other hand, if you do share my Christian worldview, you may also share my nasty habit of conflating learning for living. It's easy to read books and listen to sermons believing we're becoming more Christ-like versions of ourselves. We assume there's some process of divine osmosis happening behind the scenes. But unless we start living differently – in a way that makes people stop and think, "Well, that seems strange..." – we still have much work to do.

time to get weird

~ our quirks make us relatable ~

Our quirks are what make us loved, and how we know we belong to God's family. Just like an artist who signs his work, we all match how God prefers to work – in ways that seem a little strange and unexpected to other people.

———————

I found one of my lifelong friends, Dave, because he was short, and I was short too. When I say short, I mean *really* short. I stood a whopping four foot, nine inches, on the first day of my freshman year of high school. To put that in perspective, the average stature of my fellow freshman was a full twelve inches taller than us.

I couldn't help but lock eyes with the only other guy who shared my line-of-sight. We might as well have been walking around the first floor while everyone else wandered around the second. While we felt ignored by our peers, we felt seen by each other, and we shared a similar outlook on life so we became fast friends.

After solidifying our friendship, we began to find that our vertical challenge could be an asset. For example, we discovered we were just small enough to fit inside our school's lockers. As Dave would stuff himself inside one, I'd position myself a few yards down the hallway. Then, we'd wait for a victim. English teachers were the perfect target for pranks. One in particular was very sweet but totally gullible. As she carried a stack of papers down the hall one day, I tapped on the row of lockers and sent an echo down to Dave. After my signal he counted to five and burst out of the locker. He timed his jump so perfectly we knocked our poor teacher clear off her feet in fright. She hit the ground shrieking and sent her papers flying.

Moments like these solidified our bond. We found shared activities and he never judged me as being less-able, which is how I felt when I looked at the athletes. I always wanted to play on the football, basketball, or soccer team, but I couldn't. When I felt discouraged or uncomfortable with who I was, I'd look for Dave.

I still look for the short kid in the crowd. I try to associate with people who look like me whether I'm picking a seat on an airplane or walking into a backyard barbecue full of people I don't know. I think we all look for the "Dave's" in our lives, too. We're most comfortable around the people who like what we like, and look how we look. We steer clear of the people who seem strange to us.

Sociologists call this "finding our tribe." It's a throwback to the days when people lived in small villages of family and friends. People who looked like you were safe. If they wore the same clothing and war paint, they were alright. Anyone who didn't was a potential threat. That mindset has been ingrained in us ever since.

For better or for worse, these instincts still influence how we relate to each other. But now that the days of spears and swords have passed us by, there's a lot to gain by moving past our tribes and sharing what makes us different. You see, we always create stronger, more authentic connections when we share our quirks and idiosyncrasies. It's what makes us relatable.

Of course, shared interests are fine conversation starters. But if we crave real and genuine friendships – which I believe are in high demand in a culture driven by social media – we need to get a little weird. It's the great paradox of relationships; it's our quirks that make us lovable. The unusual and embarrassing traits we usually prefer to hide bring us together.

Think about it. The stronger your relationship with someone, the weirder the trivia you can answer about them, right? I know that's certainly the case in my life. So, when we find ourselves craving more human connection, and our close friends are the people who know the intimately-odd things about us, why shouldn't we share what seems strange about us with strangers?

Here's what I mean. You already know I'm shorter than the average male, but did you know I wear a backpack everywhere? Even if there's nothing in it. Because who knows? I might need it. I also have a thing for plain Greek yogurt. No sugar, nothing. Sometimes I put it in ice cream cones, other times I spoon it right from the container. I take icy-cold showers so my clothes feel warmer afterward. I wear earplugs at concerts because I'm convinced I'll lose my hearing early in life. I'm also sensitive to smells. I can tell you what you last cooked in your kitchen based upon the scent; seasonings, side, main course, and wine pairing.

My point is that although we can be tempted to figure out how we fit in, life's better when we stick out. We relate to the people who are more peculiar than put-together, and that's by design.

―――

Jesus once listed out all the ways in which God's design for our world is a little backward. It's recorded in one of his longer teachings, the Sermon on the Mount, and today, we refer to this list as the "beatitudes." There are eight in total, and they include statements like, "Blessed are those who mourn, for they will be comforted," and,

"Blessed are the meek, for they will inherit the earth." (Matthew 5:4-5) Every one of them cut against the conventions and customs of Jesus' culture.

His lists and stories have always been interesting to read, but I often find them frustrating. There are days when I wish Jesus would have just given us answers instead of parables. Straight talk instead of riddles. I'm sure his disciples felt equal parts frustration and confusion too. They must have elbowed each other when he began talking about a farmer scattering seeds on rocks, thorns, and a path, whispering, "Where's he going with this?"

One time, after Jesus finished a story by saying, "Whoever has ears, let them hear," his disciples had had enough. They decided to ask him outright, "Why do you speak to the people in parables?" (Matthew 13:9-10) He replied:

> *Because the knowledge of the secrets of the kingdom of heaven has been given to you, but not to them… This is why I speak to them in parables: Though seeing, they do not see; though hearing, they do not hear… But blessed are your eyes because they see, and your ears because they hear. For truly I tell you, many prophets and righteous people longed to see what you see but did not see it, and to hear what you hear but did not hear it. (Matthew 13:11,13,16-17)*

Jesus let them (and us) in on a secret. He said God created a world that only makes sense through him. So, when we try to find truth through our own methods (our eyes and ears), or through our own wisdom (the "prophets and righteous people"), we miss the big idea. It goes right over our heads. God hides his wisdom behind a veil of strange-sounding parables so that unless we follow him in a relationship, we'll never get it.

We'll always see and hear, but we'll never truly *see* nor understand. Just like the disciples who literally walked in Jesus' footsteps and learned to follow his example one day at a time, he's invited you and me to follow him. Slowly but surely, Jesus wants us to look at life from a different perspective. He yearns for us to discover that the most meaningful and satisfying parts of life feel a little strange at first, and that's intentional. They're reserved for those who aren't scared off by his quirky sayings.

This is a wonderful invitation for those of us who've ever felt a little awkward, unsightly, or abnormal. God created a world that's fit for misfits. We may not all be the short-kids-of-freshman-year, but we're all off in one way or another, and those quirks are how we know we belong to God's family. Just like an artist who signs his artwork, we all match how God prefers to work – in ways that seem a little strange and unexpected.

trespassing for the view

~ no plan is the best plan ~
When it comes to creating meaningful relationships, no plan is often the best plan. Memories and human connections are too brittle. They can't be forced to fit our molds or they'll crumble under pressure.

Have you ever lost control while driving on a snowy or slippery road? Where the backend of your car fishtails, and you can't help but wonder, "How's this going to end?" Years ago, I remember thinking, "This ain't good!" as Dave's car skid through six inches of snow, sideways, towards a cement curb. I grabbed the door and braced for impact. Curbs feel like military-grade barricades when you're unintentionally sliding toward them. As the inevitable happened, we slammed the curb so hard it snapped the car's control arm, leaving the front wheels of our front-wheel-drive vehicle immobilized.

In full disclosure, we'd chosen to drive through a blizzard just so we could slide through abandoned side roads. It was fun. When we were in control, that is. Paralyzed and helpless, it was no fun waiting in the cold for a tow truck to arrive. As the sun set and we spent our third consecutive hour sitting in the car, I wondered how expensive our twenty minutes of fun would turn out to be.

Whether it's losing control of a car, a career, or anything else in life, losing control sucks. It sucks because we love feeling we can influence the direction and outcomes of our lives. It's why we spend so much time creating plans. Plans provide us a sense of certainty and predictability. Even the most spontaneous people create plans. Type B folks just create shorter-term plans with less warning. They still expect events and experiences to develop like they envision.

The main issue with our love of plans is life rarely unfolds like we tell it. Have you noticed that? For example, you might demand your manager notice your creative genius and promote you, but that doesn't mean it'll happen. It's why for every book written about making it big and achieving your destiny, just as many pages have been written about taming anxiety and finding inner peace.

The second issue is that humans are complex. Study after scientific study concludes relationships are central to living happy and meaningful lives, yet relationships are combinations of our unique emotions, spirits, hopes, fears, and identities.[1] When all these intricacies coalesce, relationships can't fit within the orderly cells of spreadsheets and rulebooks. You can calculate if your earnings go up or down each year, but it's far more difficult to measure whether your in-laws like you more or less after the holidays.

Simply put, life is complex, and it doesn't always go according to our plan. I think that's okay, however. I'll go so far as to say when it comes to what defines our lives, our relationships, not having a plan *is* the best plan.

Now, before your inner Type A cries out, let me explain. Did you know paintings rarely turn out like an artist imagines in their head, before getting started? Paintings, music, books. All art changes with each small brush, note, or keystroke. An artist learns from the paint or print impressed on the canvas or page and from there, they know how to direct their next stroke a bit differently. The result is something far more beautiful and creative than the original vision.

Similarly, we may have a preferred vision for the future, but our desires and dreams evolve over time. We can't truly know what's best for us down the road. We only learn it by living. This is a good thing too, because while we hate to feel we've slid out of control, memories and human connections are too brittle for our structured plans. People can't be forced to fit our molds or they'll crumble under the pressure. The best plan, therefore, is often no plan at all.

Married before thirty was never part of my plan. I always assumed if I wanted to do big things, I'd have to cram them into the decade before a wife, kids, and a mortgage. I was mistaken of course, but I didn't know it until I was ready to marry my bride.

When I first started dating Erin, my wife, I was skeptical. I assumed spending time together would throw a wrench in things. At the time, I was focused on my own goals. I was building a company, racing Ironman triathlons, traveling, and generally doing the things I thought ambitious twenty-somethings should be doing. I had a timeline, and I was going to stick to it.

Erin is very pretty, however. Worse, she was interested in doing the things I liked doing. This was an irresistible combination. After she signed up to race in a local triathlon with me, I figured there couldn't be any harm in training together. We started meeting on the shores of Lake Michigan to swim at 6 a.m. every Wednesday morning. What guy can resist a beautiful girl and his favorite sport?

No man, that's who. So less than two months later, I threw the whole, "I'm just really focused on my career," line right out the window. There was one specific night that convinced me. It was the night Erin and I were trespassing in one of Chicago's city parks located across from the famed Ferris Wheel. I thought I was trying to find a better view of the city's icon shimmering in the moonlight, but I ended up discovering that Erin is worth far more than all the plans I had created for myself.

I looked down at my texts. "Great! Thanks!" Erin wrote. "I'll drive so we can park at my office downtown."

Chicago's famed Ferris Wheel was getting an upgrade. It would be taken down and replaced after a final weekend of offering free rides to the city. Erin really wanted to go but hadn't found anyone willing to go with, so I offered to join.

"Sounds good. I'm going to nap for thirty minutes, then I'll meet you out front," I tapped out. It was late, I was exhausted, and yet, I'd not only agreed to go out, I was excited about it. Something had changed. Most nights, I was in bed by 9:00 p.m. sharp. It kept my days running on schedule. Tonight, I was taking a nap to be ready for a midnight outing.

In the two months before this particular night, Erin and I swam in Lake Michigan together. We cycled through the forest preserve. We raced a triathlon. But never had we seen each other just to see each other. Oddly enough, that meant something to me. I tried to nap but instead, I thought about why this night felt significant. Surely, it was no big deal. We were just friends, right?

Thirty minutes came and went as I restlessly waited for Erin's text. My phone buzzed right on time and I scrambled down the stairs from my loft to the street. "Hey!" Erin said as I climbed into her Jeep.

"Ready?" I asked as she turned onto Lakeshore Drive.

"Very," she nodded. "I haven't been to the Ferris Wheel in ages."

As it turned out, neither of us were ready for a four-hour-long wait. By the time we arrived, there was an endless line of people snaking through Navy Pier, the Wheel's iconic home. "I was not expecting that," Erin groaned.

"I don't mind waiting, if you want to?" I offered, secretly hoping she wouldn't ask me to wait in that eternal line.

She shrugged. "I don't think it's worth it. Do you?"

"Nope. We need a new plan."

"Fine by me. Any ideas?"

"Food," I said. There's never a bad time for food in my opinion. "There's a good Mediterranean place close by, with huge portions."

A little while later we were sitting in a corner booth, managing some small talk as we browsed the menu, mostly studying each other. Each of us wanted to figure the other out. Unbeknownst to me, Erin had been hoping I'd take her on a real date, in real clothes – not another swim date in wetsuits – this whole time.

Meanwhile, my thoughts centered on what to do after we ate. The flutter I felt as I climbed into Erin's Jeep told me I didn't want to be "just friends." Friends eat and say goodnight. People who are more than friends linger. They find ways to avoid saying goodnight. I hadn't planned anything, however.

Besides, I was uncertain of whether Erin was even open to a relationship. I didn't want to force it, and if I suggested something too overt, like chocolate fondue for dessert, it'd seem inconsistent. People don't go from swim caps to sexy food inside the same week. So we settled on just wandering around for a while. After our waiter returned to the table, I quickly handed him my credit card. "I'll get this one. You can get it next time," I told Erin.

Bellies full, we started roaming the city. Without an agenda, we eventually found ourselves in the place most familiar to us, Ohio Street Beach, where we'd meet to swim. We stood on the sand looking at the same water we'd jumped in just a few days earlier.

"The Lake is way creepier at night," Erin remarked, pointing at the boundless, featureless abyss that is Lake Michigan after dark.

"Sure is. The Ferris Wheel is way cooler in the moonlight though." I pointed at the towering, signature wheel located a few blocks south from the beach. "I bet the view is even better from over there," I mused, referring to a fenced off waterfront park built between the beach and Navy Pier.

"I bet. Too bad the park's closed. We'd have to like, climb the fence or something," Erin laughed.

"Good idea. I bet the fence built inside the waterline is pretty short. We could probably climb over it."

"Nate, I was kidding."

"Oh. Well, we'll only have to go like, thirty yards down the water. We can ditch our shoes. It'll be worth it."

I'm not exactly sure how I convinced Erin. Maybe it was like one of those movie scenes where I said in a real deep voice, "When you look back on your life, how do you want to be remembered?" Regardless, a few minutes later, barefoot and soaked in lake water, we scaled the fence protecting the park. We ran to the center and stood, side by side, gazing at the bright white lights and the Ferris Wheel's red spokes rotating against a midnight backdrop.

"Totally worth it," Erin whispered.

It was a moment so special we didn't need to say much. My heart was beating so fiercely I thought Erin could hear it, which was odd because I'd climbed my fair share of fences. I'd been given a free ride home in the back of a squad car. Clearly, trespassing wasn't to blame; it was who I was trespassing with. While it's cheesy, I remember looking from the Ferris Wheel to Erin's glowing smile and thinking to myself, "Forget swim dates. I want this view."

―――

Jesus knows we love plans. He was always well aware we like to take matters into our own hands. So while he encourages us to be good stewards of the resources God entrusts us with (Matthew 25:14-29), he also tells us not to worry about even our most basic needs. In one of Jesus' most well-known but least-practiced sermons, he said, "Therefore I tell you, do not worry about your life, what you will eat or drink; or about your body, what you will wear... Can any one of you by worrying add a single hour to your life?" (Matthew 6:25-27)

Jesus shared his rationale for why we should follow his command (worrying about our everyday needs won't prolong our lives), but surely, if there's anything in life we should plan for, it's the basic necessities, right? Strangely, he doesn't say that. Not even the most essential, sustaining elements of life are worthy of our focus in his mind. In fact, the Greek word he chose to use here is often translated as "take no thought of."

Instead, Jesus chooses to divert our attention to something far worthier. By starting his command with the word "therefore," Jesus refers us back to his previous command in his prior teaching:

> *Do not store up for yourselves treasures on earth, where moths and vermin destroy, and where thieves break in and steal. But store up for yourselves treasures in heaven, where moths and vermin do not destroy, and where thieves do not break in and steal. For where your treasure is, there your heart will be also... No one can serve two masters. Either you will hate the one and love the other, or you will be devoted to the one and despise the other. You cannot serve both God and money. (Matthew 6:19-21, 24)*

This might seem easier to say before the era of 401K's and college savings plans. But by coupling these teachings together, Jesus is saying we need to shift our thinking and planning from what's in this life to the afterlife. He understood our attempts to control usually follow our cravings. We create plans around our desires. We design our lives according to what our hearts aspire to and our minds aim for. Since none of us have the capacity to "serve two masters," Jesus says we need to ditch the planning and focus on just one thing – our relationship with our Heavenly Father. In turn, that relationship will provide everything we need, including our everyday basics and our deepest longings.

Of course, this is really difficult to practice. Especially in our culture. We spend years acclimating to influence. We plant the seeds of control as we mature personally and professionally. We earn larger incomes, build stronger reputations, and we develop beloved hobbies. All of which are good things, but like thick green ivy that's pretty to look at when it's contained, our own interests, freedoms, and abilities can quickly become weeds that choke out everything else around it.

At the end of the day, God's design for our lives will be far more fulfilling than anything we could design for ourselves. I know my life with Erin after that night has been far better than everything I had planned for my single self. So, while we all hate to feel we're losing control, would you trade your sense of control for a richer relationship with God? Do you trust it'll be worth it?

the path to the top

> **~ lift others up, and you'll find yourself on top ~**
> *Ever since life in the Garden, we've wanted equality with God. We've craved top-of-ladder status. And while we've been busy climbing to the top, Jesus has been asking, "Whose feet will you wash today?"*

———————

Most of us know the biggest event in cycling each year, Le Tour de France. The yellow jersey donned by the Tour's lead rider is a sports icon. However, most don't realize the extent to which strategy and teamwork determine the outcome to this epic, 21-stage race. While athletic prowess is certainly necessary for success, without eight riders of a team – the "domestiques" – all working to propel the ninth – the team leader – to victory, nobody gets a share of the cash prize. Michael Barry, a retired domestique who supported some of the biggest names in cycling, describes this:

> *The team director plans a strategy for the stage and each of the riders has a specific role to play. For example, some domestiques will be saved for later in the day. They will stay on the wheels of their team-mates all day and then attack hard towards the finish to split up the race and put the leader in a*

> *position to win the race. Other domestiques are involved earlier on in the race, keeping the leader protected, making sure he is well-fed, swapping wheels if he has a puncture, or helping him back to the front after he stops for a pee. The main thing is just how big a factor drafting is within cycling: conserving energy is always crucial. If the strongest rider in the race wastes his energy, he won't win.*[2]

At every turn, domestiques sacrifice themselves for the good of their leader. It's a sport that values and builds its strategy around selflessness. The beautiful thing about this is when the team lowers itself to elevate their leader, in return, they all win. It's tradition for the leader to split his prize money in recognition of his teammates' essential roles.

For this very same reason, selfishness isn't tolerated in cycling. If the leader begins riding for his own glory, taking unnecessary risks and spending his energy for a few minutes of limelight in the short-term, he'll quickly be rejected by his team. Cyclists know there's no path to the podium if one teammate elevates himself above others.

It's a sport that embodies a strange but universal reality. When we lift others up, we find ourselves on top. Conversely, when we try to get ahead and put ourselves first, there's an equal and opposite effect. We only push others down, and nobody wins.

"Your new backpack looks good on you," I said as Erin hoisted a pack over her shoulder. "It's almost as big as you."

"It fits all my ski gear, thank you very much!" Erin swept by me and headed to our departure gate from the airport security area.

We were flying to Colorado for an extended, holiday weekend. A few friends were meeting us there to hit the slopes and celebrate

Erin's birthday. She was thrilled. While I always look forward to weekends on the mountain, birthdays are a big deal to Erin. So much so that in her world, everyone celebrates their "special day." That's the day of the month on which you were born, which means you get eleven extra mini-celebrations every year.

Erin marched ahead of me as we navigated the chaos of traveling during a long holiday weekend. A different kind of commotion descended on the terminal as meandering families replaced the business travelers' precise power walk. I realized I was only contributing to the disorder when I glanced up from my phone and stopped just shy of a moving walkway. I sidestepped a stroller and looked around.

"Nate, are you working right now?" Erin frowned as I looked down at my phone again.

"Nate?" She repeated.

"What?" I questioned, innocently.

"You almost took out that lady with the stroller. And I was asking if you're hungry, but you never answered."

"Are you working right now?" She repeated.

"No. Well, kind of," I replied. "I'm just texting. I guess we're getting pretty serious about this acquisition."

Another, larger company was interested in buying the startup I'd joined as co-founder just a handful of years ago. Although we were a relatively young company, we'd developed a service that was the perfect complement to our suitor's software. Talks of buying us had escalated quickly in the last two months.

I looked back to my last text from Brian, my co-founder. *Can you fly to D.C. on Monday? Might need you there to talk about the sales process.*

"Well that's exciting, right?" Erin inquired.

"Yeah, it is. They're pretty well known," I said casually.

I thought about texting back for another distracted moment. I recognized I was flying out to a birthday celebration, not just a ski trip. But at the same time, birthdays come around every year. How often does an entrepreneur sell a company? This could be a once-in-a-lifetime thing!

Definitely, let me know when I need to buy a ticket, I texted back.

A critical factor to whether the acquisition moved forward was if our future parent company believed we could sell our service to their customers. I was leading our sales operation at the time, which made me fairly central to the discussion. Naturally, the thought of me, a young twenty-something, helping to sell a startup company went straight to my head. I could see the headlines in *Entrepreneur* magazine. The interviews, the full-page features in my future. *Boy wonder does it again.*

Of course, it was possible that schedules would come together such that no trip to D.C. happened that week. I was also well aware this was a special weekend for Erin, so I decided to stuff my phone into my pocket and keep quiet. If Brian texted the meeting was on, I was certain I'd go in a heartbeat (a major personal and career milestone was at stake, how could I not?), but I'd cross that bridge when I came to it.

The next morning, I woke up with a nagging thought which said I wasn't playing my cards right. If I got the green light to fly to D.C., and I never mentioned the possibility to Erin, she'd likely feel I had hidden something from her. That, I figured, would be much worse than me actually leaving early, or me sharing plans she didn't like but didn't ultimately pan out.

I broached the topic while we pulled on our ski gear, hoping the news would mix into the stir of boots, gloves, and snow pants. "Hey, just a head's up. I might have to fly out a little early," I said as gently as I could muster.

"Excuse me?" Erin snapped up from buckling her boots. "You might have to fly out? What does that mean?"

I explained that while I wasn't sure of the meeting schedule, I may have to join Brian in D.C. on Tuesday morning. If I was needed there, I'd have to fly out on Monday. I expected her to understand, and even feel excited for me (again, how often does one sell a company?).

"Why can't you just say no? My thirtieth birthday is Monday. That only comes once," Erin pointed out, incredulously.

"Yeah, but we can celebrate another day," I reasoned. In my mind, birthdays were a mile marker you could simply pick up and move around. I was failing, miserably, to see it from Erin's point of view.

"No, Nate," Erin said firmly. "That's not the same. How long have you known you might need to travel?"

"Since Friday. But I didn't want you to get upset so I didn't mention it. Like this!" I said it as if she'd just proven my point.

"Why wouldn't I get upset? You know what birthdays mean to me. So if you leave, I'm leaving too. I'll spend my day back home."

In the moment, my ego prevented me from truly hearing what Erin was saying. If birthdays were important to her, and she was important to me, then her birthday should have been important to me too. She was making a wholly reasonable request – that I'd put her interests above my own for one day of the year – but I was deaf to it. All I heard was my imaginary phone ringing with journalists requesting interviews from the hottest entrepreneur around.

Erin turned away and pulled her goggles on. They started to fog with the steam of hot tears sliding down her cheeks, and I could hear her sniffle as we shuffled toward the door. In less than two minutes, I'd gone from a caring boyfriend planning a memorable birthday, to a conceited beau prioritizing his business.

That's the issue with climbing the proverbial ladder. In the short-term, you feel you're getting ahead. Everyone seems to be looking up at you. The reality, however, is they're not looking up at you. You're looking down on them. As we try to lift ourselves up we only push others down, and nobody likes to feel belittled. Whether it's your birthday or just a regular weekday, nobody responds to the people who quash their hopes and needs. So ultimately, those who try to get ahead will find they're all alone, with nobody to give them a hand up when they need it most.

At first, I just wanted Erin's tears to stop. I wasn't a monster, so I couldn't keep climbing my ladder if she was weeping down below. And truthfully, I didn't want to feel incompetent. What kind of self-respecting, loving person is okay with making their significant other cry? In other words, I was still concerned with myself, never seeing Erin as my priority.

It took me some time, but as we sat in the lodge eating our lunch, my thick head finally grasped what was at stake. I'd come to a critical turning point; whether I stayed or left would be a signpost for Erin, signaling which direction I wanted our relationship to head. Would I place Erin above my own ambition? Or would I get ahead at all costs?

I slid down the bench of our lunch table and whispered, "Erin, look, I'm really sorry. I wasn't thinking. Well I was thinking, but only about me. I won't leave even if the meeting happens."

"You mean that?" Erin tested me.

"Yeah, I really do. And I think you're going to like what I have planned for your birthday."

The meeting in D.C. did ultimately happen, and Brian handled the conversation for me. While I didn't get a seat at the proverbial table, let alone my news interviews, I came out on top. Erin and I had a great day snowshoeing to the peak of a Colorado mountain, and now, she knows she comes first in my life.

In Jesus' era, the Jews hoped and prayed for a liberator. The "Messiah," the anointed one, was supposed to deliver them from Roman rule. Visions of sweeping military defeat and a hero's cape flowing in the wind filled children's dreams at night. But when Jesus appeared on the scene, he didn't fit the vision. He didn't seem like a liberator. He seemed lame, and far too tame.

Instead of stomping on the Romans with military strength, Jesus strolled in, "humble, and mounted on a donkey" (Matthew 21:5). Instead of elevating himself over Caesar as a domineering king, he described himself as "gentle and lowly in heart." (Matthew 11:29). He never assumed the Roman throne and he was born in a manger (the modern, urban equivalent of being born in a bus shelter or alleyway).

This wasn't because Jesus was powerless. In fact, it's precisely because he possessed supernatural strength that he was able to embody true humility. Jesus was the only person throughout history who *could* have had his way at any moment. With a spoken word or flick of the wrist, Jesus could have indulged his desires – his fully human desires. Even when Satan came to him after forty days and nights of fasting and said, "If you are the Son of God, command these stones to become loaves of bread," (Matthew 4:3) Jesus never used his power to alleviate his own suffering or address his own needs.

Instead, Jesus knew he'd been sent to serve, and to lift up humanity through brutal sacrifice. He told his disciples exactly that. "[T]he Son of Man did not come to be served but to serve, and to give his life as a ransom for many." (Matthew 20:28)

Jesus served in countless ways that seemed strange and totally counter-cultural. For one example, I run a lot, so my feet can get pretty sweaty. I've lost toenails and I've grown warts. Despite all this, my feet are lovely and sanitary compared to the downright-disgusting feet of our ancient relatives. Cuticle scissors and antifungal hadn't been invented, and people walked scores of miles in dirt, dust and open-toed sandals. Nevertheless, Jesus assumed one of the nastiest jobs a servant could be assigned – washing feet:

> *When he had finished washing their feet, he put on his clothes and returned to his place. "Do you understand what I have done for you?" he asked them. "You call me 'Teacher' and 'Lord,' and rightly so, for that is what I am. Now that I, your Lord and Teacher, have washed your feet, you also should wash one another's feet. I have set you an example that you should do as I have done for you. Very truly I tell you, no servant is greater than his master, nor is a messenger greater than the one who sent him. Now that you know these things, you will be blessed if you do them. (John 13:1-17)*

This sequence of events is just incredible. Consider it for a moment. The all-powerful creator, who owes us nothing, sends his son to earth. Jesus doesn't only walk the earth as part of the divine Godhead. He shares in the worst of our humanity. Extreme hunger, filthy servitude, and crushing sorrow mark his life. In all this, he does more than preach at us. He cleans our feet, then suffers for us. He assumes the lowest, most humiliating form of death possible.

And wouldn't you know it? As he lowered himself, he raised up humanity. He bore the punishment we deserved, freeing us. To revisit

Paul's writing on the topic, paradoxically, he says Jesus' humiliating death actually made him greatest of all. While reinforcing Jesus, "…made himself nothing by taking the very nature of a servant, being made in human likeness," Paul continues to say:

> *And being found in appearance as a man, he humbled himself by becoming obedient to death — even death on a cross! Therefore God exalted him to the highest place and gave him the name that is above every name, that at the name of Jesus every knee should bow, in heaven and on earth and under the earth, and every tongue acknowledge that Jesus Christ is Lord, to the glory of God the Father. (Philippians 2:6-9)*

In his final act, Jesus finds himself on top after lifting others up. It's a definitive example that cuts against our oldest, deepest desires to get ahead. Ever since life in the Garden, we've wanted equality with God. We've craved top-of-ladder and cover-of-magazine status. And yet, while we've been busy climbing to the top, Jesus has really been asking, "Whose feet will you wash today?"

my life in a duffel bag

~ this life is just preparation for another ~
I'd been overlooking the fact waiting is part of what it means to be human. There's more to come after this life, so living with a low-grade feeling of suspense isn't something we're supposed to get past. It's something we're supposed to stoke.

I follow a certain routine every time I check into a hotel. I set my duffel bag on the desk, slide my shoes underneath, lay tomorrow's clothes on the chair, and I look to see if I'll be charged $14.99 for the water bottle near my bed. I know I'll only be in the hotel for a short while, but I travel so often (more on this in a bit) it's nice to start settling in. It lets me know I've arrived, that I'm no longer in transition.

But suppose after settling in, I went out and bought a new TV for my room. Not just any TV, an 80-inch, ultra-high-definition display. Then suppose that on my way back, I had one of those Tempur-Pedic mattresses delivered to my room. Which would of course require me to upgrade to silk sheets. And I couldn't do all this without swinging by the local art gallery for an original Impressionist piece to tie the room together.

If I were to actually do this, you'd say I lost it. You'd see my checkout date in two days and assume I was an absolute loon. Even if I'd just won the lottery and thousands of dollars was of no consequence to me, it wouldn't be worth the effort. People don't invest that kind of time and money into what's here one minute and gone the next.

Yet, every day we prioritize our pursuits in this life over preparing for the next, that's exactly what we're doing. We're upgrading our hotel room even though we're just passing through. We may not know when our life's "checkout date" is, and it could be a while from now, but we do know the death rate in our world is 100%. A valuable question, then, is how should we use the time in our "hotel room?" In the context of eternity, what's the most meaningful way to spend our few short days?

I mentioned I travel a lot. If you recall that business meeting I didn't attend so I could be with Erin on her birthday, you'll recall that the point of the meeting was to determine if a Washington D.C.-based company would buy our Chicago-based startup. Well, one month later, they did. This, in turn, meant I'd need to move to our nation's capital.

I started traveling to D.C that spring. My home was still in Chicago so I'd fly to D.C. on Monday, fly home on Friday, and repeat. By the summer, I knew I had roughly six more months of traveling between cities before I'd need to officially move to D.C. I also knew I loved Erin, so we got engaged that summer and we started planning our wedding, move, and new life together.

So began the season of my life that was supposed to be my highest of highs. I'd made a big career move, I was marrying my love, we were starting a new adventure together. But instead, I spiraled to an all-time low. I felt empty, restless, aimless and anxious.

It became too expensive and impractical to keep my Chicago loft while traveling every week, and we'd soon be moving cities, so I lived as a modern nomad for this eight-month stretch of my life. I moved from couches to futons to air mattresses with just a bright green duffel, a sleeping bag, and my laptop in tow. I'd accept whatever accommodations were offered to me, including those which came with leaking roofs and squeaking mice. I rarely stayed in one place for more than a handful of days. I didn't always know where I'd land next, either. That included cities, as one month before our wedding, our company allowed me to pick Denver as our new home. I would build our business out West, while Erin and I built our life in the mountains we loved.

My life on-the-go was an energizing adventure at first, but a draining chore by the end of it all. I became a hollow shell of myself, aimlessly drifting from couch to couch like a leaf floating down a stream filled with sticks redirecting its path. While I should have spent the time preparing for my married life to come, I was too wound up and strung out.

The gravity of how poorly I was processing this season of life crushed me on the most juxtaposing of mornings – Erin's bridal shower. All of Erin's friends and family gathered to celebrate her, as I walked into the room reeling, like I'd been sucker punched then kicked in the teeth.

Bridal showers are pretty typical. Most women have them. Most women receive gifts. I was not aware of this. I'd never been to a shower, so I was told to just show up near the end, say hello, and pick Erin up. My first shower experience didn't play out like that, however.

"Hi, I'm looking for my wife. She's having her shower here. Do you know where that's at?" I asked one of the staff members standing at the front of the country club.

"Yes, just down this hall and the room is on your left."

"Thanks," I smiled and started down the hallway. The soft buzz of women chatting began to crescendo, telling me I was on the right track.

I stepped into the room and froze, immobilized by what stood in front of me. Wide-eyed, I stared at two long folding tables filled with beautifully-wrapped presents. They covered the entire tabletop. It was more stuff than I'd seen in the last half-year of living from a duffel bag. Though they stood at a height of three, maybe four gifts tall, they looked like small towers looming over me.

"Nate!" Erin motioned for me to come over to her. She sat in a white chair apart from everyone else. There was a second, empty chair next to her.

"We're going to open up presents together," she explained as I cautiously approached the front of the room.

I took my assigned seat as a waterfall of consumer goods rushed over me. My collar felt too tight. My heart raced and my palms dripped with sweat. Could I fit all this in our car? It certainly wouldn't fit into my duffel bag. And even if it could, then what? I had no home to bring it to. What kind of future husband has no home to welcome his bride into?

The waterfall gave way to waves of panic breaking over me. My breathing grew ragged and my mind raced. It was like I'd stumbled into my own intervention. I knew I'd been suppressing anxieties I should have been processing during this season of life as an itinerant, and to be fair, I've never liked clutter, but this was another level of unnerving. It was a legitimate panic attack.

"Oh! This one's from me," someone called to Erin as a gift was placed in my hands, and the harassment began. I gave it to Erin and tried my best to smile like a happy fiancé would.

I continued my charade masking my panic for the rest of the event. I preferred to conceal my feelings, not confront them, but it wasn't easy to hide from Erin. She knew me too well.

"Are you okay?" She asked me later that night. "You've been kind of quiet today."

"I'm..."

I tried to say I was fine. Just tired. It was a well-rehearsed excuse at this point, but my words came out like I'd just gulped down a pint of sand. Choppy and painful. I couldn't keep faking it; I collapsed in a puddle of tears like a child worn thin from a full day of shopping.

"Oh, Nate," Erin sympathized as she started to calm me down. "It's okay to keep crying," she encouraged. "It's just me here."

———

What I couldn't explain to Erin in between my sobs was that I felt like someone had pressed pause on my life. I was in a season of waiting, which by definition meant everything was not yet as it was supposed to be. I had no address, no home, no rest, and the anticipation was killing me. I was moving toward all I ever wanted – a successful career, a beautiful wife, a new city filled with new opportunities – but the longer I waited, the more drained I felt.

What I'd been overlooking was the fact that waiting is part of what it means to be human. Weddings, careers, and everything else on earth for that matter aren't supposed to fill us. There's more to come after this life, so living with a low-grade feeling of suspense isn't something we're supposed to get past. It's something we're supposed to stoke. It's a reminder that lets us know we're still on our way home. C.S. Lewis described this in his seminal work, *Mere Christianity*:

> *If I find in myself a desire which no experience in this world can satisfy, the most probable explanation is that I was made for another world. If none of my earthly pleasures satisfy it, that does not prove that the universe is a fraud. Probably earthly pleasures were never meant to satisfy it, but only to arouse it, to suggest the real thing. If that is so, I must take care, on the one hand, never to despise, or to be unthankful for, these earthly blessings, and on the other, never to mistake them for the something else of which they are only a kind of copy, or echo, or mirage. I must keep alive in myself the desire for my true country, which I shall not find till after death; I must never let it get snowed under or turned aside; I must make it the main object of life to press on to that country and to help others to do the same.*[3]

Incredible. *The most probable explanation is that I was made for another world.* In an eternal context, my waiting wouldn't stop once Erin and I got married and moved cities. All of this life is just "living in a hotel room."

It's remarkable how many times the Bible references this. For example, Jesus referred to himself as a groom waiting for his bride. (John 2) Later, we're told to "stay dressed for action" just like "...men who are waiting for their master to come home from the wedding feast." (Luke 12:35-36) Paul said "creation has been groaning as in the pains of childbirth" as we wait for our new life that's to come. (Romans 8:22)

Typically, we associate any length of waiting with wasted time. We loathe visiting the DMV. We buy fast passes to skip lines at airports and amusement parks. We sigh when we hear we're the tenth caller in the queue. And do you know what? Jesus' followers weren't any different. They assumed Jesus came to build a physical kingdom, and "they supposed that the kingdom of God was to appear immediately." (Luke 19:11) But as we've seen time and time again, Jesus did the opposite of our expectations. He didn't build an empire. He remained homeless for all intents and purposes, living on futons, camping pads, and air mattresses. He even said, "Foxes have holes, and birds of the air have nests, but the Son of Man has nowhere to lay his head." (John 18:36, Matthew 8:19-20)

The time we spend waiting for life in God's kingdom doesn't have to be wasted, though. In fact, it *shouldn't* be wasted. While a landlord wants us to avoid putting holes in the drywall and turn his property back like we found it, God calls us to a higher standard. He calls us to invest, multiply, create, and cultivate what we're given.

Jesus described this call through the story of a rich man who moved overseas. Before he left, he gathered his workers and "...gave them ten minas. 'Put this money to work,' he said." (Ten minas is equivalent to three months' pay, which is no small amount of money.) Later, when he returned, "...he sent for the servants to whom he had given the money, in order to find out what they had gained with it." The first servants share they've earned ten and five additional minas respectively, and he's elated. He rewards them with more trust and cities to govern. Then, the next servant comes in and hands back the same amount to him. No holes in the drywall, exactly how he left it. What do you think happens next?

> *Then he said to those standing by, 'Take his mina away from him and give it to the one who has ten minas.' 'Sir,' they said, 'he already has ten!' He replied, 'I tell you that to everyone who has, more will be given, but as for the one who has nothing,*

even what they have will be taken away.' (Luke 19:11-27)

Not what you expected, right? It seems strange Jesus would take everything from the one who had nothing. Isn't Jesus about grace and giving? Here's the thing. God is incredibly serious about how we prepare ourselves for life in his kingdom. Instead of spending our days strung out on the future, sitting and waiting around for his return, he's concerned with how we're living today. What we do on earth echoes into eternity, so we're called to live with purpose here and now, preparing for there and later. Paul says, "[W]hether we are at home or away, we make it our aim to please him. For we must all appear before the judgment seat of Christ, so that each one may receive what is due for what he has done in the body, whether good or evil." (2 Corinthians 5:6-10)

So here's the point. We might have a home and a place to lay our heads at night, but we're not home yet. We're all just living out of a duffel bag. A life of waiting often feels draining, but God meant for it to serve as our training. This is a time to prepare for the day he'll finally welcome us home with rest for our weariness, peace for our anxieties, and a place we'll fit in forever.

the time I almost went to court

~ we can be right and wrong at the same time ~
*Jim was no longer someone to love, he was someone to beat.
An obstacle standing in the way of me standing in the right.
However, I'd been in the wrong all along. While I believed playing
my trump card meant I'd won, really, I'd just revealed my hand.*

I spend most of my weeks trying to be right. At work, at home, with friends, with family. It feels good to be in the right, doesn't it? Whether it's a mechanical question like, "How do I know if my car's burning oil?" or a relational question like, "What do I say to my grieving friend?" it's nice to have the answers. Competency is among the most satisfying feelings. To feel competent is to feel skilled, wise, accomplished, trusted, and sought after, all in the same moment. Who doesn't like that?

In fact, I like to be right so much that sometimes, I make stuff up. It's probably the one thing I do that embarrasses Erin more than anything. I'm a terrible actor on camera, but on life's stage, I'm an Oscar winner.

For example, as Erin and I were hiking on a sweltering summer day, we took a water break on the trunk of a fallen pine tree. I opened my pocket knife and started to peel away some of the bark. As I chipped away, a middle-aged woman with the personality of your fifth-grade lunch lady emerged from a bend in the trail. Immediately, she fixed her eyes on my carving.

She approached me, folded her arms, and chided, "Hey! You shouldn't be harming that tree. Stop!"

I looked up from the trunk, partly bewildered and completely uninterested in being told I was wrong. Picking at a decomposing tree wasn't hurting it, right? I held my tongue and hoped she would move along. A moment later, she quipped with biting sarcasm, "What are you, some type of botanist?"

Seeing no National Forest Service patches on my critic's outfit — much less any justification for chastising me — I decided to turn the tables on her.

"Why yes, I am," I said without skipping a beat. "I'm studying the cohabitation of plants and insects at Texas A&M. The high sierra beetles have really decimated this region, so I'm trying to establish cause-of-death for this spruce. Are you aware of the beetles in this area, mam?"

"Oh, well, no. I'm not," she apologized.

"That's surprising. They've grown pretty aggressive in recent years," I continued my charade. "We're just hoping that with enough research and early action we can stop the spread." I glanced at Erin as she buried her face in her hands, mortified.

"Have a nice day," the lunch lady groaned as she moved up the trail.

Once she was out of earshot, Erin lifted her head to comment, "Nate! I can't take you anywhere!" She wasn't thrilled, but I was quite pleased with my performance. I smiled wider than a kindergartner holding a fishing pole hooked to a six-inch bass.

Somebody tried to back me into a corner and I emerged the

victor. I was in the right — even if I'd made some (or all) of it up. The irony of my botanist impersonation is my need to be right often finds its root in Imposter Syndrome.[4] It's the shadow cast by my driven, ambitious personality. Imposter Syndrome is a pervasive fear that someday, I'll be found out. The world will discover that any accomplishment I may have once claimed was happenchance, the mere byproduct of sweet serendipity. I suppose one can have a healthy dose of Impostor Syndrome, like a glass of red wine. I overdose, however. Getting drunk on accomplishment numbs my feelings of inadequacy. I can't be condemned if I'm on the king's throne, so figuring out how to be in the right proves to be a coping mechanism.

The trouble with this is that always trying to be right is like bringing a treadmill to a marathon — it gets you nowhere. It's a hopeless endeavor without an end. Life's a long race, and more often than not, we all make mistakes. "Be right" is a Sisyphean goal. "Do right, don't be right," is a far better mantra I've tried to adopt. "Do right" lets me screw it up, as long as I make it up.

I share this as context to the time I was both right and wrong in the same moment. I was equally correct and mistaken while embroiled in a dispute with a negligent contractor. To set the stage a little further, Erin and I had just bought a home. It had been one year since we moved to Denver, and being a first-time homeowner was exciting. Replacing junction boxes and hanging cabinets are, perhaps surprisingly, all things I enjoy. I like figuring out the answers to life's issues. I feel capable when I do, so buying a house was like a playground full of problems to solve and opportunities to feel good about myself.

After we closed on our house, we gave ourselves one month to complete all the major renovations that would be easiest without furniture standing in the way. Flooring and painting, in particular. We ripped up carpet late into the night. I hauled cases of flooring from our local Home Depot. But when it came to painting, it was going to be too big of a job for us to complete before our move-in date. The yellow-and-green color scheme definitely had to go, so I invited four different painters to give us an estimate.

One of the painters, Jim, stuck out to us. He was willing to go the extra mile without billing us for time spent on small projects. Jim explained he was a new business owner, and his crew was very experienced, so if he didn't keep them busy with new projects, he couldn't retain them. I could empathize. We talked about the plight of growing small businesses and that sealed the deal for me.

"The guys are going to be excited to hear this," Jim smiled. "When do you want us to start?"

―――

Jim and his crew finished painting on a Thursday evening, so Erin was planning to see the new blue-grey colors after work on Friday. However, a blizzard hit Denver that morning and locked her in our apartment. I was in San Diego visiting my brother, so I wasn't around to brave the snow and see the house either.

The snow cleared up by Sunday morning, and as I waited to board my flight back to Denver, Erin called. "Nate! Nate!" her voice cracked as I slipped on my headphones.

"E, what's up?" I wasn't sure if she was panicked, or if there was static in our connection.

"Icicles are hanging from our faucets, and all the toilets have ice blocks in them!"

I froze in the middle of the airport walkway. "What? How's that possible?" My mind raced, considering the possibilities. Our house temperature had dropped while I took a few days to set up our utility services, so I was positive I'd set the thermostat to a balmy seventy degrees before I left for San Diego.

"Our windows are wide open! The heat's turned off!" she cried.

This was Jim, I thought to myself. *Why would he do that?*

"There's paint smeared in the bathtub, and it's speckled on the kitchen island too — I'll send you pictures. Nate, this had to be the painters," Erin confirmed my suspicion.

Erin was panicked because frozen pipes mean burst pipes, burst pipes mean floods, and floods mean moldy drywall, warped hardwood, thousands of dollars and months of restorations. I looked at my watch as I thought about what to do. My flight was boarding soon.

"Just hang tight. This is Jim's mess. He needs to fix it." I called Jim after I hung up with Erin but I didn't get an answer. *Answer your phone,* I texted before calling again.

Jim picked up on my second call. "Jim, it's Nate. Listen, your guys left our house a mess. The windows are wide open and the heat is off. Our pipes are frozen solid."

"How's that possible?" Jim said, genuinely shocked. "My guys don't leave a job site like that."

"Well, they did. Had they not left paint smeared around the house, I might have believed you."

"I just, I can't believe that."

"Jim, Erin's at the house crying, scared of flooding. I need you to get over there now."

"Okay, yes, I'm on my way."

―――

Jim had left our house by the time I arrived from the airport. I didn't bother to drop my backpack, I just walked from room to room, watching ice melt from our P-traps and faucets. Erin and I sat on our stairs, waiting for a plumber and wondering what would become of our new home. I really, really didn't want to replace soggy drywall.

"Hello? Oh hey, I'm T.J. I hear you guys have some frozen pipes?" T.J. the plumber said as he walked through the front door.

"Yes, hi T.J. Thanks for coming."

"No problem. I'll make sure you're not in any immediate danger tonight, just checking everything out visually. Then I'll come back tomorrow when I have all my gear so I can run a full inspection." T.J. said as he started walking the house.

A little while later, T.J. reported back. "So, based on what I'm seeing, which unfortunately I see all the time, I'm guessing the toilets and faucets are cracked, exposed piping will need to be spliced and replaced, and we'll see about damage to piping inside the walls tomorrow."

"Best case," he continued, "I'm guessing two, maybe three thousand in damages. I'll let you know more tomorrow. Have a good rest of your night," he offered as he stepped outside.

I chucked my backpack into Erin's trunk and sank into her seats. "We're not going to wait for the bill to file an insurance claim," I said, processing my thoughts aloud. "This is negligence. It's on Jim's insurance," I said firmly, digging out my phone to call him.

Jim answered immediately. He was anxious to hear the latest news. I relayed T.J.'s opinion and asked for his contractor's insurance. "I need you to email me your policy tonight," I directed him. I was going to do it myself to ensure it got done and we stayed on schedule with our renovations. "I want to get repairs started this week."

"Of course, I'll work with you on this," Jim assured me.

"Great. I realize this isn't the position you want to be in, either."

Jim hadn't sent me his insurance information by the next morning, so I called him as we drove back to our new house. T.J. would be finishing up his final inspection soon.

"Listen, Nate, you know I want to work with you on this, right?" Jim started off in a smooth voice. "But after thinking about it, I just don't see this as my fault. Really, you guys should have gone to the property to make sure everything was okay."

He was starting to slip the ropes of responsibility. "Hold on Jim," I cut him off. "You can't have this both ways. You can't tell me you'll work with me, but then say it's my fault."

"Well, what I'm saying is I'll guide you through the process, but I can't file a claim on my policy. It's not my fault. My guys don't operate this way, and even if they did, you're responsible for your own property now. This is your home."

A tidal wave of vitriol swelled within my chest. I knew exactly what Jim was up to. He wanted to avoid increased insurance premiums. The path to saving his neck was convincing me, a first-time home-owner, that I'd missed part of my job description. Then, after sufficiently convincing me *I'd* shirked *my* responsibility for *my* property, Jim could play the rescuer. He'd swoop in to negotiate costs with the plumber and guide me through the rehab process.

I was fuming, but I kept as composed as I could. "Jim, stop. Let me make this very clear. This is on you. If you try to wiggle out of it, I promise this will end even worse for you. Neither of us want to go to court, but if we do, there is no scenario in which you walk."

I'm sure Jim felt the knife-edge in my voice. Erin, who prefers to avoid direct conflict at all costs, felt it. She was staring at me, wide-eyed.

"Woah, Nate, I told you I'm going to work with you. Court's not going to be necessary."

"I hope not. Because this is on you."

"Well, I don't believe a court will see it that way if it goes there," Jim snorted.

I laughed before shooting back, "Here's the headline, Jim. 'Negligent contractor takes advantage of unsuspecting homebuyer.' How do you think that's going to go?"

"I think they'll see things my way," Jim dug his heels in.

"Let's just see what the damage is and we'll take it from there." I hung up the phone.

T.J. sent me his invoice two days later. Miraculously, the final bill for the inspection totaled a mere $525. T.J. said that in his twenty years of plumbing experience, he'd never seen pipes freeze and leave zero trace of damage. Our pipes were completely intact, and none of the porcelain in our toilets or sinks had cracked. They were as strong as ever, in fact. It was a literal miracle.

I expected Jim to respond to my texts sharing the good news. Instead, he didn't reply and started screening my calls. Jim dodged me for weeks, ignoring my repeated requests to pay T.J.'s invoice, which began to accrue late fees. After a month of no response, I switched my approach. I was in Nevada for work, so I picked up my hotel phone and dialed his number. "Hello, this is Jim," he said.

I smiled. "Hi Jim, it's Nate. We need to talk about an invoice."

Jim groaned, "Nate, that was your plumber. I won't pay."

"I hoped we could avoid this Jim, but I don't feel we're going to agree on this. Can we at least agree on that?"

"Yes, agreed. You and I are far apart on this," Jim granted.

"Okay, then I'll be filing papers for a small-claims suit tonight. You can expect notice of a hearing in the near future."

Feeling confident that I was in the right, I was leaning into Jim, hard. I wasn't going to let him paint me as the inept homeowner. "By the way, when I file those papers, the total won't be $525. You'll be paying damages for mental anguish, lost income, and it's going up on every review site out there."

I was in control of the situation, and I knew it. I wanted Jim to admit that he was wrong, I was right, and there was nothing he could do about it. This was no longer about rectifying contractor negligence – this was about me feeling like I was back on top.

"Nate, I can't keep talking about this, I have work to do," Jim said as he hung up.

Expecting this, I cracked open my laptop. I'd already drawn up papers to file my claim. I pressed "send" on an email I'd drafted to really put the screws to Jim. I'd had an Ace of Spades up my sleeve the whole time. With a little research, I'd discovered that Jim's ex-wife was listed on the LLC's state registration. So, I named her in the suit, demanding she show up to the hearing too. Picture that for a moment. Can you imagine Jim defending himself, with his ex-wife forced to stand with him?

Here's the thing. Did I think I was brilliant? You bet. But was there evil in my heart? Unfortunately. I'd suppressed the little voice telling me to *do* right – to treat Jim respectfully and show him grace – instead of trying to *be* right. In fact, I'd flushed the whole *do right, don't be right* mantra right down my fully-intact toilet.

As I walked through the airport that day, Jim was no longer someone to love. He became someone to beat. He was an obstacle standing in the way of me standing in the right. However, I'd been in the wrong all along. While I thought playing my trump card meant I'd just won, really, I'd just revealed my hand. I'd shown my true colors.

If I told you I was compassionate, but the only interaction you'd observed was that of me and Jim, you wouldn't believe me. My behavior said it all. Sanctimonious, smug, and coarse. Far from graceful.

Love Does author Bob Goff says that, "Burning down others' opinions doesn't make us right. It makes us arsonists."[5] Bob's right. Jim proved I fit the profile of arsonist. If I'd been holding a big enough match, I would have burnt his business to the ground. I genuinely enjoyed the fact that I'd found leverage and emerged victorious. In the same way, arsonists enjoy watching flames lick over the homes, vehicles, and forests they set ablaze. It's why they do it – there's pleasure in it.

This all sounds really ugly, doesn't it? Well, Erin thought so too. Once she learned how I was twisting Jim into submission, she questioned whether I was approaching things in a way I'd regret. Confronted, I tried to put lipstick on the pig. I layered on pretext like, "If he'd do this to us, who's next?" and, "I'm just protecting the other homeowners he's going to screw over!"

Erin pointed out how I'd forgotten what I'd learned (let alone what Jesus commanded) through many screw-ups of my own. It's one of the many reasons we go together so well; Erin smothers the matches that only stand to do me and others harm. She was right. While I may have been legally correct — Jim was responsible for the damages — I wanted to be right, not do right, and that made me wrong.

I'm sometimes tempted to feel Jesus' stories are irrelevant to modern living. I mean, if Jesus had been party to a contractor's dispute, he would have told him to pay up, right? While Jesus talked a lot about loving people, saying things like, "Do to others as you would have them do to you," does that really apply to forgiving debts? (Luke 6:31)

Yes, it does. In fact, Jesus spoke specifically about forgiving debts. (Matthew 18:21-35) He told the story of a man who owed a bunch of money (about $7.04 billion worth in today's dollars[6]) and had his *entire* debt canceled. But immediately thereafter, the same man went out and demanded payment from another man who owed him just a few hundred bucks, saying "Pay back what you owe me!"

This man had a right to the "hundred silver coins" he was demanding. He was technically owed that money, so "he went off and had the man thrown into prison until he could pay the debt." He drew up the papers, placed a call, and took the legal action he knew he could. But while his actions were legally permissible, were they truly *right*?

The original lender who cancelled his debt didn't think so. When the lender learned what the forgiven man had done he said, "Shouldn't you have had mercy on your fellow servant just as I had on you?" In other words, he was pointing out that although the forgiven man was right in one sense, he was wrong in the ways that actually matter. Consequently, the lender had the unmerciful debtor jailed and punished.

When we're mistreated, we do have the right to seek justice. But when we go about it in the wrong ways, we not only ignore the billion-dollar forgiveness Christ already extended to us, we miss our best opportunities to demonstrate gratitude and grace.

Paul wrote, "Love is patient, love is kind... it is not self-seeking, it is not easily angered, it keeps no record of wrongs." (1 Corinthians 13:4-5) He knew love is something we live out, to reflect the love God shows us. Similarly, John wrote, "[L]et us not love with words or speech but with actions and in truth," because when we do, it's

"[H]ow we set our hearts at rest in his presence." (1 John 3:18-19)

When Erin called out my actions as unloving, my heart wasn't at rest. Sin is unsettling at a soul level, and I was clearly acting in the wrong. It's uncanny how closely Jesus' story aligned with my situation. There I was, no better than the man who owed billions, demanding my lunch money from Jim while assuming I'll be shown grace for my own missteps when we "give an account of ourselves to God." (Romans 14:12)

I wish I could say I acted counter to our litigious culture, forgiving Jim's debt to stick out as one of Christ's followers. I did ultimately pay the plumbing invoice and drop my claim, but if it wasn't for Erin's gentle nudge toward Jesus' way, I'm not sure how this story would have ended. Thank heavens for my wife.

It may be you've never bought a home, or you've bought one, but never found yourself entangled in a contractor dispute. Nevertheless, maybe there's a "Jim" in your life. Is there someone you could call or text to say you were wrong, even if you were "right?" If there is, take it from me. No relationship – not even hired help – is worth burning for the sake of being right. It's better to do right and stick out for Christ's sake.

living life in a tunnel

~ the more we give, the more we gain ~
When we give away love and we spend ourselves for others, we ultimately find there are more people out there who love us. It's simple – loving people find themselves loved, and selfish people find themselves living in dull, lifeless tunnels.

———————

Erin and I like to hike the Rockies. Before we hit the trail, we sit and sip coffee. As we enjoyed our coffee one morning, I started editing a section of this book. I became so engrossed with editing that when Erin asked, "Can you make some sandwiches to bring with us?" I said, "Sure," without actually hearing what she had said. I knew she said something, but I was too focused on my own project to process it. After I set my computer aside, I knew I had missed something important.

"What do I need to do again?" I asked.

"Sandwiches," Erin said flatly.

"Oh, right." I walked over to the fridge to gather supplies. When I looked inside, there wasn't a single slice of bread, turkey, or cheese to be found. "I can't make sandwiches," I stated. "We don't have any meat or cheese."

"Are you serious?" Erin moaned. "I laid everything out next to you. The ingredients are *literally* right in front of you."

I turned and sheepishly looked at the table. Sure enough, Erin had spread the necessary sandwich-making provisions around my computer. It was a serious case of myopia. I wish I could say this was atypical, but unfortunately, we have a few exchanges like this weekly, if not daily. Selfishness is to blame. My tunnel vision usually stems from me refusing to part with what I treasure, like writing books. I love writing. It feels good to finish a big project and tunnel vision gets me to the end fastest. I fly right by other people's needs and requests; the scenic route of conversations and sandwiches just slows me down.

Tunnels may be fast, but they have their downside, too. Living inside them makes for a very bland existence. There's not much to see or do inside them. There's just a lot of cement and fluorescent light, which is true of the Eisenhower Tunnel we drove through on our way to hike that day. Although it's the longest tunnel and highest point on the U.S. Interstate system, driving through it doesn't involve anything more than watching gray walls and smelling exhaust fumes.

By contrast, the Eisenhower's alternate route, Loveland Pass, takes you up and over the Continental Divide. The views are stunning. During the winter, the highway is carved into the middle of massive ice walls so it looks like Santa Claus' driveway. If the Pass' 11,990-foot elevation doesn't take your breath away, the uninterrupted, sweeping views of snow-capped Rockies surely will.

So, if tunnels are boring and Loveland Pass is beautiful, why choose the tunnel? Well, as with most things in life, there's a choice and a tradeoff. To get the Pass' iconic views, you have to give up the tunnel's convenience. Similarly, in my life, if I don't give up my own projects to do little things for those I love (making sandwiches), life would be pretty plain. Ironically, I wouldn't have much to write about.

All of life happens to work this way. We're naturally inclined to choose the fast-track to our own goals, desires, and comforts, but when it comes choices as simple as driving through a tunnel or as complex as marriage, the more we give, the more we gain.

A bender of nonstop work travel recently triggered a particularly acute case of my tunnel vision. I'd flown to Minneapolis, Milwaukee, Seattle, San Francisco, and D.C. inside of two short weeks. Most people fatigue as they spend time away from home but I pick up speed. You know that law in physics, "an object in motion tends to stay in motion?" That's me, an object in motion. The more I work, the more I want to work. The more I travel, the more I want to travel. The further I drive into my work tunnel, the more the people in my life look like sandwich ingredients. Right in front of me, totally unnoticed.

By the time I was headed home from the airport, I was picking up steam on a direct collision-course with Erin's needs. We collided when a few friends asked us to meet them at a brewery. I wanted to go. An object in motion, remember? Erin, on the other hand, went ahead and declined for us. She said we were going to spend a night home together.

"We'll have plenty of 'us time' this weekend," were the first words out of my mouth when I dropped my bags at our front door. "Tonight works for everyone. Let's go out."

"Everyone but us," Erin quickly reminded me. "I've seen you on one day out of the past two weeks. I miss you."

"But we'll be together tonight," I reasoned. I had spent the last two weeks directing my own schedule, you see. I worked, explored, and dined as I pleased. For whatever reason, I figured tonight shouldn't be any exception. Erin could come along for the ride as I defined the stops on our itinerary.

"That's not the point," Erin said. "I was hoping you'd want to spend time with me."

I should have seen caution signs appear at this point, but I just kept driving down my tunnel. Beyond my desire to direct our schedule, the efficiency of it just made sense to me. Inside a single day, I could see my colleagues, wife, and friends, going from boardrooms to breweries. Besides, if we were together, why couldn't we also be with others? The more the better, right?

I said as much to Erin. "Of course, I want to be with you. But if we go out, I get to spend time with you *and* friends. Isn't that better?"

"I don't think you're hearing me," Erin said patiently. "I've been in our house, alone, for two weeks. Now you're here, but you don't want to be alone with me. How do you think that feels?"

To be honest, I wasn't thinking about Erin's feelings. I knew what I wanted and I'd started down my tunnel days ago. So, I kept barreling forward. "I do want to be with you. *And* I want to see our friends. I can't see them when I travel, you know."

I thought that last line would seal the deal.

"You can't see me either," Erin countered. "Besides, you're always traveling, so I was looking forward to tonight being just us."

The message wasn't getting through the tunnel's concrete walls. I was still hung up on going out. It was what I wanted to do, with the people I wanted to see, and that only made Erin look like a roadblock.

That feeling only intensified as she added, "You have to choose me sometimes."

Choices entail sacrifice. Intrinsic in a choice is the reality you can't have it both ways; you have to give up at least one of your options. I wasn't interested in forgoing my plans however, so I pushed back, again. "That's not fair."

"Fair?" Erin asked, surprised. "What's not fair is not being able to put me first once in two weeks."

I'd reached the end of my tunnel. I was out of road so I snorted, "Fine, we'll stay home," and dumped myself onto our couch. I tried to look bored. If I was forced to stay in, it would become an act empty of my heart. I wanted to have it my way but the night unfolded in such a way we were both left with nothing. My defiance twisted our options into either dismissing Erin's needs, or locking me away in a cage. I'd created my own *Kobayashi Maru*.

The solution was pretty simple, too. Had I considered Erin's point of view, I'd have realized she enjoys nights with our friends just as much as I do. She also knows it's good for us to reconnect after spending weeks apart. There's value in prioritizing our marriage, even if it means sacrificing a night out. That's fairly obvious even to those who aren't married. Healthy relationships can't blossom when we put our interests over the other's. If I wanted a thriving marriage, something had to give.

I knew this deep down. Nevertheless, there are moments in which I can't see outside my tunnel's walls. To atone the next day, I decided to write Erin a letter. You'll soon learn I write Erin a lot of letters, but this was a different kind of letter. It was a letter of resignation addressed to my company. It explained that my travel had taken me away from my family too often, so I was giving up a good position in a growing company.

I didn't mail it, however. Walking away isn't always the right answer. Sometimes, we simply throw good things out of balance which turns them bad. Instead, I addressed it, stamped it, and handed it to Erin. It was my way of saying I'd made my choice. I'd give up my travel to gain our relationship, if she so chose.

It's easy to miss what we have when we're focused on getting more. It's the great lie of our age. We kill ourselves to make a life, believing we'll only start living after a little more. A little more status, wealth, or experiences. The truth is just the opposite, actually. The more we give, the more we gain.

It's one of the great paradoxes Jesus spoke about. He regularly said things like, "If you cling to your life, you will lose it, and if you let your life go, you will save it," and, "Give, and you will receive. Your gift will return to you in full — pressed down, shaken together to make room for more, running over, and poured into your lap." (Luke 17:33, 6:38 NLT)

This is very encouraging if you think about it. Jesus is basically telling us, "Look, the most important thing on this earth, *your life*, it's actually the easiest thing to get. You just have to let it go. There's no ten-step plan. Just give it up." These are my words, not his, but you see the point.

Jesus is able to say this because he didn't only *prefer* us to be the kinds of people willing to lay down our lives for our friends (our enemies too, actually). He believed in this way of life so strongly that he lived it out, to an excruciating end on the cross. He didn't die because it was best for him. He knew we'd never live perfectly loving and generous lives – ones deserving of eternity – so he did what was best for us. He paid the penalty that was ours to pay, and in so doing, he graciously offered us a relationship with his father.

Our choice to receive that grace and live in relationship with our heavenly father is also a choice to accept Jesus' call to lay down our lives. We're called to echo his example by spending ourselves for the well-being of others. As Dietrich Bonhoeffer said in his book, *The Cost of Discipleship*:

> *The cross is laid on every Christian… the cross is not the terrible end to an otherwise god-fearing and happy life, but it meets us at the beginning of our communion with Christ. When Christ calls a man, he bids him come and die.*[7]

Wait. Come and die? Really? That's not exactly the line you lead with if you're trying to build a multi-generational movement of people set out to change the world. Wouldn't it have made sense for Jesus to offer something a little more, approachable? I mean, if I'm throwing a house party and I want people to actually show up, I'm not going to say, "Make sure you get a good night's sleep and come alert. You'll probably die on your way over. It'll be worth it, though."

Yet, as we see time and time again, Jesus spoke in ways that turn our expectations upside down. His invitation to live sacrificially and love generously, even to our own peril, is his way of saying, "I'll provide." He wants to provide us a *truly* valuable life, one worth far more than any life lived for our own ends.

To return to Bonhoeffer's words, "Christianity preaches the infinite worth of that which is seemingly worthless, and the infinite worthlessness of that which is seemingly so valued."[8] Here's an example of this. If you walk into work one day and your boss says, "You're being promoted with a twenty percent salary increase, and if you do well, we'll double it next year," all of us would be elated. Ever since our first career or college fair, we're accustomed to working for more status, earnings, and opportunities. They seem to hold immediate worth. On the other hand, when it comes to spiritual things like love, joy, peace, patience, and kindness, they seem worthless. How is joy going to pay the bills? The neighbors won't be jealous when I show off just how patient I can be, will they? But Jesus (and Bonhoeffer) tells us these morals are of far greater value.

We know this is true because if one day you decide a doubled salary and all the status in the world hasn't fulfilled you, you can't trade them for contentment. What once seemed to be worth so much can't buy you what you really long for – joy, peace, and meaningful relationships. These things are too valuable. They can't be bought. Instead, we only get what's truly valuable by giving first.

The reality is when we give away love and we spend ourselves for the good of others, we ultimately find there are more people out there who love us. It's simple. Loving people find themselves loved. Selfish people end up living in dull, lifeless tunnels.

crying while flying

~ considering death creates a better life ~
Considering my death on that late-night flight brought us more than a final letter for Erin. It gave us a richer life. It brought me a stronger love, here and now.

Erin sees my writing before anyone. Her memory is sharper than mine, so her feedback develops each story I tell. While she recounts our relationship's memories from her perspective, without fail, she always offers the same piece of advice. "You shouldn't be so hard on yourself. You look like the bad guy, and I look like an angel."

I'll give that to her. Since most stories I tell are about the lessons I've learned, naturally, my screw-ups are on display. I will give this to myself, though. There are many weeks in which all I want to do is love my wife and make sure she knows she's the most beautiful person in the world.

One of these weeks began with Erin crashing into our bedroom in a panic yelling, "Nate! Nate! I can't find them!"

"Huh?" I asked through a mouthful of toothpaste. It was early on a Monday morning, and my mind was full of conference call agenda items. "You can't find what?"

"My letters! I wanted to re-read my dad's letters, and when I went to grab them, they were gone."

Before Erin's father passed years prior, he authored a number of letters to her. Some were hand-written, others had been transcribed while he was sick. They mean the world to her so she's incredibly intentional about where she keeps them. As we started to move into our new house, she'd bundled them alongside every love note I'd penned. Counted together, they represented more than one hundred notes composed over seven years. If there's any single item Erin could choose to save in a house fire, it would be her box of letters.

"Oh, well I'm sure they're around here somewhere. When was the last time you read them?" I asked.

"Before we moved," she groaned. "What if we threw them out or left them behind?"

"No way," I answered categorically.

"How can you be so sure?" Erin challenged.

"Well, let's go through the whole house and all the boxes in the basement before we get too worried. Okay?"

"Okay," she agreed. "But you know how much those letters mean to me, right?"

I nodded. She wasn't convinced I fully understood so she started to say, "Me losing my letters would be like you..." before pausing to think of a potent-enough comparison. "Well, it would be worse than you losing every single one of your possessions."

"That would be bad," I nodded once more.

"Yes, it would be. So please help me find my letters!"

I trotted down to our basement to comb every cardboard box that had sat idle since our move. Fortunately, there were only a handful of boxes to search. Neither of us like clutter. Unfortunately, after ten minutes of hunting, I was convinced Erin's letters weren't in our basement. "Let's look again tonight," I offered in a cheerful tone as I emerged from the stairwell. "Maybe we just need to start over with fresh eyes."

"Yeah, okay," Erin conceded as she fought back tears.

A fruitless night of searching came and went. Although I wouldn't let it show for Erin's sake, I was genuinely considering the possibility I'd thrown them out by mistake. It crushed me to feel I might be causing her so much anguish.

We returned to scouring every nook and cranny in our home the next morning. I re-searched the same places I'd examined just ten hours earlier, doing everything to avoid accepting those letters' dreadful fate. As I started to consider how long it would take me to re-write one letter for every relationship milestone we'd shared, I heard Erin cry out.

"Nate! Nate! I found them!"

Erin sprinted into our bedroom clutching a box of pancake mix. Apparently, I love pancakes so much I figured a box of mix would be the safest place to stash Erin's most valuable possessions. Tears of joy and relief welled up in her eyes. She hugged that box like a mother who'd lost her child in the middle of Times Square.

"They're still here," she whispered through tears.

I sat down and hugged her. "They're still here," I repeated.

———

Work called me away the following morning. I spent the next few days on the road so by the time I was headed home, I was beyond ready to see Erin. Her pretty brown eyes were all I thought about while boarding my late-night flight.

I put on my headphones as we rolled down the runway and were lifted into the night sky. I watched Philadelphia's sparkling city lights fade to black, and marvelously, as we climbed higher and higher, the soundtrack to our wedding's first dance switched onto my playlist. Suddenly, I felt as if I'd been transported to the set of a Hallmark movie. Time stopped and the sounds of my wedding sucked me into a world where I was the only passenger aboard. I almost believed all hundred musicians of a full-scale orchestra were serenading me from the last twenty rows.

Hot tears threatened to slide down my cheek. My mind scrolled through memories of our relationship as if I were shuffling through a stack of letters. Each memory felt as present as the bag of pretzels I was handed a few minutes later.

I'm told crying is healthy. That it's a cleansing experience, kind of like sweating out the emotions trapped inside you. I've tried to cry in the past to see if that's true, but it never worked. This time, I didn't need to try to cry. It just happened.

As the sounds of our wedding faded and my tears subsided, the words I'd want to say to Erin in the last moments of my life came into focus. I'm not sure if the search for Erin's letters inspired them, but whatever the reason, my life's final words held my mind captive. I felt this intense, indescribable need to write them down. It was like I was in fact dying and therefore, I *had* to record those words. I was in a race to write them out before my hands stopped working.

Even now, I don't feel I'm able to sufficiently communicate just how surreal an experience this was. I really thought I was having some sort of pre-death premonition. The possibility of an early demise became my reality that night, so I could only think about writing. Knowing how much Erin loves her letters, and this would be my last, what more could I do?

I felt her next to me as I scribbled down my thoughts. Strangely, I felt no fear. I ignored thoughts of my death in favor of spending my last hour consumed by her love. Eventually, I leaned back in my seat and wiped my eyes. If that night was to be my last, at least I'd leave one more note behind.

Regardless of how and when I go, considering death on that late-night flight brought me more than another letter for Erin. It brought us a richer life, here and now. Recalling that experience reminds me to fill my days with love while I still have time; it's the only thing I'll be concerned with in my final moments.

The best example for how to live and love richly is found in the one who conquered death. Jesus knew a wooden cross would cut his time on earth short, so while he didn't live long, and his years in formal ministry were relatively brief (about three, according to most historians), he made every year count. He spent his time with the forgotten, the outcast, and the loveless. He served, taught, and traveled with the people he wasn't supposed to be seen with. He took an interest in thieves, prostitutes, and the mentally ill. And strangely enough, he focused his time on just twelve disciples, none of whom had remarkable backgrounds.

When you think about it, loving a small and estranged group of people is an odd way to live if your life's purpose is literally "savior of the whole world." If you knew death was near, wouldn't you focus on influencing as many of the most prominent people as possible? Yet, Jesus' strategy of loving his small circle worked out. His disciples got the message, and they went on to deliver God's love letter to our world, the Bible.

A part of that message is the shared source of purpose behind our and Jesus' lives. John wrote in his gospel, "For God so loved the world that he gave his one and only Son [Jesus], that whoever believes in him shall not perish but have eternal life." (John 3:16) Do you see what John's saying here? He's saying God believes you are of such eternal worth that he chose to sacrifice his *one and only son* for you. If the purpose of Jesus' time on earth was to bring you into relationship with God, what does that say about how much he loves you?

When we reflect this immeasurable love through our lives, we find our days become far richer than when we live for any other end. If you're not convinced, consider the alternative. Thomas Nagel's *The Meaning of Life* describes the death we'd all have to live in light of while speaking of a reality in which there is no God:

> *...it wouldn't matter if you had never existed. And after you have gone out of existence, it won't matter that you did exist. Of course, your existence matters to other people – your parents and others who care about you – but taken as a whole, their lives have no point either, so it ultimately doesn't matter that you matter to them.*[9]

Fortunately, the whole point of Jesus' message is that our lives have a point. So much so that in God's plan, your life is worth his son's death. While Jesus rose again, that doesn't change the tremendous cost he paid in the process. When we consider this cost, we see the value of our lives more clearly, and we find new direction for how we're to live while we still have time.

Just think. If you didn't have time to write it in a letter before you go, will those around you know they're loved? How much more rewarding will your last moments be if you know you did your best to share His love with others while you still could?

feelings are like honey

~ the most powerful sentences contain the fewest words ~
"I love you," and, "I'm sorry," just five words total, happen to be the mightiest sentences of them all.

On the first day of my college course, "Intro to Relationships: Interpersonal Dynamics & Interaction," my professor said ninety-five percent of the time, tears should be followed by an immediate apology and hug. During the remaining five percent, the severe cases, a brief discourse that alerts the other person of an incoming hug should precede physical contact.

Just kidding. I never took a college course called "Intro to Relationships." Classes like that don't exist. It would be antithetical, in fact. As I learned while trespassing for a view with Erin, in the moment we define a series of steps for building relationships, we undermine our own end. Rulebooks kill genuine, healthy relationships. And yet, I've always wanted that manual. Directions are simple. Emotions are complex.

In fact, the renowned psychologist Paul Ekman developed six universal categories to classify all emotions – anger, fear, disgust, joy, sadness, and surprise – but within these categories are intricate layers. For example, while Ekman's team analyzed anger, they discovered sixty unique expressions of anger. Angry-frustrated, angry-depressed, seething anger, and so on. These expressions become even more complex when we use them to organize our memories. We label past experiences based upon these feelings, and it's these feelings that help us recall certain events – not the details of the moment. Think about it. You probably remember how you felt right before your first kiss, but can you recall how many chairs were in your fifth-grade classroom?

Feelings are like honey in this way. They're sticky. They don't wash away so easily. And if you've ever left a bottle of honey sitting on the shelf for too long, you know it becomes even more difficult to deal with over time. Trying to squeeze crystallized honey on toast takes longer than baking the loaf of bread.

This was my perspective on emotion in relationships. It's too complex, there's no manual, and I either end up with a soft and sticky mess, or a hardened shell that gets me nowhere. Fortunately, Erin and our chocolate lab, Belle, showed me feelings don't have to be that complicated. It's actually the simplest phrases like, "I love you," that are the sweetest and most powerful.

―――

"So, do you think you'll enjoy having a dog more, or the same, now that Belle's staying with us?" Erin asked as we jogged along a creek-side trail near our home. She was referring to the beautiful, four-year-old chocolate lab fastened to the leash I held. I wound the leash around my hand as Belle darted toward a cottontail rabbit.

Dave, Belle's owner, had landed a prestigious summer internship while pursuing his MBA, which required him to travel every week. When I told Erin that Belle needed a home for the summer, she was thrilled.

"We'll turn our house into Camp Nasralla!" She exclaimed.

Erin has these gorgeous brown eyes that make it impossible to say no. They brim with tears at the sight of a dog in-need, which only makes it more difficult. Seriously. One photo of a senior-aged dog living in a shelter elicits a more emotive response than me falling from a 12-foot ladder. That's not to say Erin doesn't love me. She just *really* loves dogs.

So, without much debate, we did open Camp Nasralla for the summer. Belle had been living with us for two months at this point, and Erin had started referring to herself as "mom." She didn't want Belle to grow confused, however, so she'd tell Belle we were a "modern family." Meaning, Belle had two dads and one mom. These are all things I should have considered before responding to Erin's question. Except I didn't. Instead, I just said what I thought.

"Less, actually. I'm less likely to want a dog."

"Wait, what? Less excited?" Erin abruptly slowed our jog to a walk. I'd taken the wind from her sails. "How's that possible?"

Belle looked backward as if to say that she, too, heard what I said, and she didn't appreciate my attitude. My statement was wholly genuine, mind you. I travel like a pilot most weeks, and those first two months of Camp Nasralla validated my assumption that arranging our calendar around a furry friend's needs would require sacrifices. I wasn't interested in making extra sacrifices.

As I focused on the logistical implications of dog ownership, I completely missed the feelings enfolded in Erin's question. There's more to communicating than the words we choose to speak, and I had overlooked how Erin chose to frame her question. Asking if I felt *more* excited or the *same* implied it couldn't be possible to feel *less* excited.

"You asked how I feel about owning a dog. I feel I'm less likely to want one," I repeated with as much sympathy as a sack of jalapeños.

I wasn't just lacking sympathy, though. I was only thinking of the burden on my schedule. I wasn't considering how much I love to see Erin happy, and how happy Belle makes Erin. Every morning that Erin wakes up to Belle excitedly wiggling her booty is like nine-year-old Erin being told it's a snow day, and school is canceled. Let the good times roll!

"You're kidding." Erin coughed in disbelief.

"No, not kidding," I said flatly.

We had reached an impasse. I jogged ahead of Belle, imploring her to follow and drag Erin along with her. It worked, and we resumed our run. It was a quiet morning on the trail. There weren't many other cyclists or joggers to distract us, so I was forced to listen to the drumming of our shoes and the swishing of our shorts. Neither of us spoke to the other.

Eventually, Erin broke our silence. "I just thought you would see how much I love Belle. You know I love her, right?"

"Of course," I replied.

Erin continued, "She's the best dog ever. I mean, Belle is *so* well-behaved. How are we ever going to get a dog if even *she* can't convince you?"

"Fair question," I pointed out.

"Yeah, it is," she stated.

We ran in silence for a few more steps before I offered, "I'm not saying 'never.' I'm just saying 'at this time' I don't feel very thrilled about owning a dog." It didn't seem to help.

———

Like we said earlier, feelings are like honey. They're sticky, and it takes more than a brief moment of conversation to manage them. And if you've ever left a bottle of honey sitting out for too long, you know it gets worse. It crystallizes. That afternoon, I let Erin's feelings crystallize. I mistakenly assumed end-of-conversation meant end-of-issue. After we left our run to go to work, she went through her day hopeless that I'd ever see the issue from her perspective.

On the other hand, I didn't see a need to follow up on the conversation. I felt justified in my response. She asked what I thought, and I spoke my mind truthfully. She wouldn't have wanted me to lie, gaslighting a scenario of doggy delight, would she? Maybe not, but my options weren't binary. Instead of choosing between a positive or negative response, I could have addressed the feelings behind her question. But I didn't.

Erin dropped her keys on the kitchen table later that evening and I looked up from my laptop to ask, "Hey, how's it going?"

"I thought about our conversation," Erin looked away from me as she spoke. She pulled a coffee thermos from her purse and set it in the sink. "I don't think we finished our discussion."

"What's to discuss? You asked what I thought. I answered."

"Yes, true. But we never talked about how I felt," Erin replied.

"Okay, how do you feel?" I inquired.

"Like I wasn't heard," she said.

"But didn't you ask me? I thought you wanted my answer?"

"Yes, but I wanted to talk about your answer. You went silent as we ran like you didn't want to talk, then we went to work."

Erin paused for a moment before continuing, "And I was expecting you to text me. Or call. You know, something to say you get me and how I'm feeling. But you didn't."

"Get me." Keyword being "me." Erin didn't say "get a dog." Erin was talking about her need to feel understood by her husband, not her need for me to love dogs. I missed that, so I said, "Oh, guess I didn't know I was supposed to."

"It's not about what you were or weren't *supposed* to do. It's about the fact you didn't *want* to know how I feel."

"But I thought this started by you asking how I feel!" I reacted.

"You're not getting it!" She cried.

"What's there to get? You asked me how I felt about a dog, and I told you!"

That's when the tears started. Erin turned away, recoiling like you do when something burns you. She stepped toward the sink and drizzled soap into her coffee mug. The running water muted her sniffles, but I didn't need sound to know she was sobbing. I didn't like that she was crying. It was uncomfortable, so I petitioned her, "Just tell me what I should do now."

"Nate!" She cried. "I don't want to have to tell you!"

I continued digging my grave. "How should I know then!"

"Just hug me! Say you're sorry!" Erin pleaded, exasperated.

I moved toward Erin and wrapped my arms around her. As we stood in our kitchen chest to chest, my first trace of relational acumen appeared as I whispered, "I love you, E, and I'm sorry. I should have said that sooner."

Erin nodded, affirming she'd heard me, and she appreciated my gesture. She never wanted to change my opinion. She only wanted to know she was heard. I stared at our dishwasher as she remained motionless within my embrace. I felt grimy, sullied for making my wife cry. I envied our dirty dishes. If only I could crawl inside our dishwasher like them, I could load in the soap and turn the dial to "Power Scrub." We'd all emerge one hour later, spotless.

People don't get to sit inside dishwashers, though. When we walk into honey and we feel sticky and grubby, there's no "Power Scrub" to wipe things clean. Instead, we only have our words. As it happens, our most powerful sentences are the easiest to form if we choose to use them. They contain the fewest words. "I love you," and, "I'm sorry," just five words total, happen to be the mightiest of them all.

———

Meaningful relationships aren't built by quid-pro-quo. "We can get a dog so long as you…" That never works over the long-term. Flat out capitulation doesn't work, either. It's only a matter of time before contempt and resentment sets in. Instead, I think a more viable alternative is to allow our desires to be reshaped. More often than I'd like to admit, I don't want something simply because *I don't want to want it*. Do you know what I mean? I develop a certain narrative in my head, and when something contradicts that narrative, I shut it down.

The narrative I'd developed said dogs kill freedom. You may laugh, or cringe, but I'm serious. My thought process went something like, "As soon as you give in and adopt a dog, say goodbye to travel, spontaneity, long weekends and late nights – all of the freedoms you love." Surprisingly, the day Erin had to part with Belle was the day I became open to Belle returning. The story I'd been telling myself started to fade like twilight in the late summer hours, and I grew open to my desires maturing.

I turned on my phone as our airplane's wheels skipped along the tarmac at Denver International one day. My screen lit up with the preview of a new text from Dave, Belle's owner.

"Hey, I'm going to have to let someone take care of Belle when I graduate. They offered me the job," it started off. "My sister can take her, so I don't want you to feel any pressure if it's not the right choice. But if Belle would be the right dog for you and Erin, we could make Camp Nasralla her new home."

I smiled. One month had passed since Belle checked out of Camp Nasralla. Each week since, I checked into a new hotel and called Erin to ask how her day was. A recurring thought shoved its way into my mind with every call I made. "Nobody is going to welcome Erin home tonight." I hated that thought. I hated that it wasn't irrational; it was reality. As it persisted, it reversed my longstanding aversion to building our schedule around a dog's. I wanted to know Erin would be welcomed home by a smiling face each evening (dogs do smile, I've learned).

I texted Dave back, "I'd say let me confirm that with Erin, but I think she'd get on a plane to pick up Belle tonight if you asked." I pasted Dave's message into my texts with Erin, followed by a "?"

She texted back immediately. Like incoming missiles, a series of seven texts communicating how much she loved Belle blew up my phone. The last one asked, "But what do you think?" I didn't need more than a few words. "I'd love it."

God's words have shaped our world since the beginning of time. A pattern originates in the creation story whereby God speaks, it becomes so, and it's good. Light, water, land, sky, plants, animals, people. Everything on earth is here because God declared it into existence, and every declaration was made to care for us. There's always been intention and provision behind God's words.

Likewise, the gospel author John calls Jesus himself "the Word." He writes, "The Word became flesh and made his dwelling among us." (John 1:14a) Incredibly, the source of life itself lived among us, talking, teaching, and speaking what we have recorded in the four gospels. When we study Jesus' words in the gospels, it's striking that he addresses more than theology. It would have been reasonable for him to spend his entire ministry correcting doctrine and amending teachings in the synagogues. The world's literal know-it-all could have very accurately called us on our spiritual crap. But he didn't do that. He did more than just preach. He was intentional about *how* he speaks and with *whom* he's speaking.

All of Jesus' interactions were deeply steeped in emotion. Not only the emotions he felt, the emotions we felt. Jesus recognized there was a specific individual with unique hopes and fears behind every issue and request brought to him. Always understanding with whom he was speaking meant he not only addressed the question, he addressed the questioner.

Zacchaeus, hurry and come down, for I must stay at your house today, he said to a lonely, isolated tax collector who needed to feel seen and cherished. (Luke 19:5)

Let any one of you who is without sin be the first to throw a stone at her, he said on behalf of a condemned, ashamed woman who needed to know she was not lesser than her accusers. (John 8:7)

In these examples and countless others, Jesus shaped his words to fit and fill the emotional emptiness at the center of who he was connecting with. As a result, though he lived in a culture of oral traditions and storytelling, he didn't need half-hour stump speeches to land his message. Some of his most impactful moments can be summarized in the single sentences we have preserved in scripture.

This is good news for any of us who have ever felt awkward or ineloquent. We don't need prepared remarks or locker room rallies fit for halftime at the championship game. All we need are short, intentional sentences focused on each other's core desires.

Imagine if you were to pull aside a shy, withdrawn colleague after a work meeting and say, "You're so brave. You worked hard on that presentation. I bet it took a lot of courage to ask for feedback." How will they feel? My guess is they'll treasure that comment over any other workplace praise. Why? It's not the presentation or product that's the focus – it's the person, and their need to feel fearless.

When we place another's needs at the center of our sentences, we don't need to add any filler. Our words are most powerful when we don't dilute them. *I'm coming over. I hear you. You're loved. You're enough.* In fact, a single, intentional phrase aimed at another's unaddressed emotion is often enough to scrub away years of feelings that have crystalized into gloom and despair.

Who needs you to speak into their life this week? What do they need to hear from you?

the best noodles I ever ate

~ small choices can bring big consequences ~
It's humbling to realize the sovereign God of the universe is also interested in managing the finer details of our lives. It's comforting to know our unknowable futures aren't left to chaos; they're guided by him who was able to set the perfect conditions for life itself.

We recently escaped an avalanche that raced down the Rockies and onto the Colorado Interstate, swallowing up cars commuting back to Denver. "Escaped" might be a little dramatic, but had Erin and I started our drive just fifteen minutes earlier, we would have been engulfed by a massive pile of snow. An unbelievable thirty inches of snow had fallen during the prior two days, which made for the perfect ski (and avalanche) conditions. We didn't want to squander fields of champagne powder, so we chose to forgo breakfast and hit the slopes early.

That tiny choice had an enormous impact on the rest of our day. Had we left just a few minutes later, we'd have been swamped by snow. Now, I can't say for certain our day turned out *better* than those who were trapped by the snow. Perhaps the avalanche was someone's snowy savior, preventing them from sliding off a cliff a few minutes later. But what I think we can say is that small choices can carry big consequences. Even routine, run-of-the-mill decisions can snowball into much more significant outcomes over time.

It's plain to see that something like signing a mortgage or proposing marriage will alter the course of your life, but nobody thinks twice about lingering over a bowl of cereal. And how could we? We couldn't function like that. Just imagine the mental energy required to get into the office on a Tuesday. Life is simpler, easier, when small decisions feel contained.

Yet, small decisions don't always keep to themselves. There's an interesting (and scary) branch of mathematics called Chaos Theory that unpacks this. Chaos Theory states a tiny change in the initial conditions of a certain system can result in massive differences later on and over time. You may have heard this called the "Butterfly Effect." That's the name a mathematician, Edward Lorenz, coined after studying a real-world example of how chaos affects our lives.

Lorenz's butterfly-based example discusses weather, and how "a butterfly flaps its wings in China and sets off a tornado in Texas. Small events compound and irreversibly alter the future of the universe... [he then refers to a line chart] a tiny fluctuation of 0.00001 makes an enormous difference in the behavior and state of the system 50 generations later."[10]

When applied to our lives, that's remarkable. We'd like to believe that our lives are built on linear cause-effect relationships. Life is cleaner when one decision produces a single and direct outcome. However, our lives are much more dynamic than this. An immeasurable set of variables coalesce to influence the trajectory of our lives, and there's a multiplicative effect when you consider we don't live on an island. Our lives affect others around us, too.

I shared earlier that most of my career has been focused on growing startups. That journey began after I'd grown weary of my job working as a consultant for a reputable, well-paying firm. I didn't feel fulfilled, and I grew disinterested in working for high-flying law firms. The security it afforded didn't mean much anymore. Instead, I wanted to watch an idea sprout into a full-fledged company; I wanted to build a startup.

To explore my options, I started setting up lunch and late-night meetings with other entrepreneurs around Chicago (my home at the time). I hadn't met Erin yet, so my focus largely revolved around work and making a name for myself in business. I kept the beginnings of a company in my sketchbook – a name, a logo, a revenue model, etc. – but I never pulled it out in the office. I figured my co-workers would second-guess my loyalty (and my sanity) if they discovered I had been ducking team outings to attend meetings with people I barely knew, to pursue an idea that, statistically speaking, was likely to crash and burn.

I tucked a sketchbook into my backpack and slipped out from behind my desk one afternoon. My co-workers had been talking about options for lunch, but I already had plans, and I preferred to leave the office without explaining them. I crept to the elevator uninterrupted, found my bike parked outside, and hopped on. I had waited until the last possible minute to leave the office, so I cranked on the pedals and weaved in and out of noontime traffic. I glanced at my watch as I came to a skidding stop outside a noodle shop. I had just enough time to lock my bike and fix my hair before spotting who I was meeting. Despite the lunch-time crowd, he was unmistakable. He looked just like his LinkedIn picture.

"Hi, I'm Brian," he rose to shake my hand.

"Nate, good to meet you, Brian," I replied.

"So, you have an idea?" He asked as we sat down at a corner table. "How can I help?"

I opened up my sketchbook and explained the concept I was working on – a platform to help small nonprofits raise money. Brian listened intently. He asked good follow-up questions, inquired about my motivations, and was genuinely curious. After I finished, he nodded, complimented my creativity, and leaned in a little closer.

"Here's my idea," he began.

Brian had been working in small nonprofits for the past decade. He knew what keeps them up at night and how they raise money. He drew a beautiful painting in my mind, connecting lines from the motivations I described to the nonprofits he knew and the platform he'd been developing. I ate my noodles and listened with rapt fascination. He wasn't just talking about a hobby or even a business. He was outlining a mission. There was an undeniable charisma and sense of purpose behind his words. I was quickly sold on dropping my idea in favor of developing his.

"You should meet the team I'm building," he suggested as I picked up our noodle bowls. "You know, ask them questions, see what you think."

"Sounds great," I agreed. "I'll email you later today."

Two weeks and two meetings later, I decided I was in. I'd dive headfirst into building Brian's idea, and I'd give my consulting firm my two-week notice. I knew it was a weighty decision to make. I was leaving a stable salary and an established firm for a significant pay cut and an uncertain future. But I didn't think of it as a truly life-altering decision. I only saw the career move in front of me, not years of major life milestones that would soon shift as a result.

With the benefit of hindsight, I can say meeting Brian for that bowl of noodles was the best choice I ever made. Through it, I found a partner who shaped me as a startup co-founder, and someone who developed me as a person, too. We've ridden out five years of ups and downs, and we've watched an idea spread to thousands of nonprofits and hundreds of cities.

Best of all, I met Erin. I had always planned to leave Chicago and head west, but the business planted me right where I was able to get to know her, start dating, and fall in love. Without that bowl of noodles, I don't think this book would even exist. It really did put me on the path you've been reading about. A while after those noodles, our company was bought, Erin and I got engaged, we moved to Colorado, bought a house, adopted a dog, and as they say, the rest is history.

It's strange to think I was one meal away from a very different life, but maybe you can relate. What's your bowl-of-noodles story? If you can't think of one, who knows? Maybe it's right around the corner.

Graciously, the trajectory of our lives isn't left to random chance. There's a divine patterning in the fabric of our lives. While the scientific revolution was supposed to expose faith as obsolete, one of modern science's most salient discoveries is how our world's natural laws conspire to uphold intelligent design. In fact, we've identified more than two dozen unique parameters that must be precisely aligned in order for our world to sustain life. The physical conditions that allow for our existence are so impossibly strict the probability of us walking and talking is equivalent to you dropping a pin from the International Space Station and hitting a one-inch target on Earth. No kidding. Every day we rise, eat cereal, and sit in traffic is so rare it's an ordinary miracle.

David reflects on God's awesome design in Psalms 8 as he writes:

> *When I consider your heavens, the work of your fingers, the moon and the stars, which you have set in place, what is mankind that you are mindful of them, human beings that you care for them? Lord, our Lord, how majestic is your name in all the earth! (Psalms 8:3-4,8)*

It's humbling to realize the sovereign God of the universe is also interested in managing the finer details of our lives. It's comforting to know our unknowable futures aren't left to chaos; they're guided by him who was able to set the perfect conditions for life itself.

What's strange to me is how God chooses to guide our lives. He has all the power in the world, yet he rarely employs loud bangs and bright lights to direct us. Instead, he uses tiny beginnings to bring about the majestic fullness of his kingdom. For example, Jesus equated his kingdom to a mustard seed, "…which is the smallest of all seeds on earth. Yet when planted, it grows and becomes the largest of all garden plants, with such big branches that the birds can perch in its shade." (Mark 4:30-32)

Most of us aren't familiar with mustard seeds but Jesus was speaking to an agrarian society, so this would have been a striking choice of parallel. The typical mustard seed is just 0.05 inches wide, but as Jesus says, with time and fertile soil, it grows up to nine feet tall. That's over 2,100 times its original size. Farmers even had to plant mustard in fields, not gardens, because a tiny seed would produce a large tree that germinated and sprouted acres upon acres of new roots and branches.

Jesus reinforced that God brings about mighty plans from small beginnings in a related parallel. He said, "The kingdom of heaven is like leaven that a woman took and hid in three measures of flour, till it was all leavened." (Matthew 13:33) Three measures was equivalent to sixty pounds of flour, so a small dose of yeast would produce a whole lot of bread.

I think a large part of what these parables mean for you and me is we don't need to worry about how our lives will turn out. Although small choices can certainly shift the direction of our lives and produce big consequences, that's how God prefers to construct his kingdom. One mustard seed and bowl of noodles at a time. All we need to do is trust God's always working to weave together his plans, and listen for his leading as best we can.

gas station milkshakes

~ we never catch the things we chase ~
Jesus said we'll never catch grace if we chase it. He didn't just preach it, either. He lived it. He gave away grace so people stopped foraging for it.

I slipped out of bed and shuffled into the bathroom. I sipped cold water and stood barefoot on the tile, feeling the chill travel through me from the bottom up and top down. My master plan wasn't working. I'd soon be starting a 500-mile drive through rural Colorado and I wanted to ensure I awoke well-rested. I figured that if I simply tried harder, if I really focused on dozing off, I'd fall asleep within a few hours of my 5:00 a.m. alarm. That wasn't the case, however.

I finished my water and pressed the little button on the side of my watch. It glowed with a dull green hue, informing me 1:00 a.m had already come and gone. I'd been lying in bed for hours thinking about sleep, but not actually sleeping. I forced myself to yawn before crawling back into bed, hoping I could trick myself. People who yawn are tired, and people who are tired go to sleep, right?

Neither the cold tile nor my yawning made me want to fall asleep. I stretched the comforter over my face and stifled a loud groan. Nothing more than a nap was possible at this point, which only intensified my desire for sleep. But of course, trying to regain lost time only cost me more time. The harder I tried to doze off, the more alert I grew. Have you ever experienced one of these nights? Where the more you try to sleep, the more awake you feel?

Eventually, I stopped looking at my watch. I knew I'd already lost the fight for a full night of sleep. That, of course, was the moment in which I finally fell asleep. When I stopped the race, I reached the finish. Strangely enough, I caught what I'd been chasing as soon as I gave up the chase.

Life can feel a lot like that night of sleep. It's like one giant game of Whac-a-Mole. You remember Whac-a-Mole, right? That game where you use a rubber mallet to smack mechanical moles randomly popping out of holes? I spend so much time and effort chasing ephemeral goals, feelings, and experiences that emerge for a limited time, occupy all my attention, and then disappear. Yet, the more I chase them, the more I feel like I'm falling behind. More and more moles continue to appear and I fear I won't be able to whack all of them before my time is up. I'm scared the buzzer will sound and I'll look up to a big scoreboard that says I should have hustled a little harder, chased a little longer.

I had a lot of think-time on my drive that morning. Five-hundred miles worth, actually. As I drove the two-lane highways curling along the Rockies like an eternal cement snake, an old friend from college came to mind, John. You see John met this girl, Carly, on a spring break trip. A whole group of my friends were there with us, but John and Carly *really* hit it off. They spent time with us, but it might as well have been just the two of them on this trip. Carly clearly and very quickly became John's "it" girl.

He was smitten with her. When we got back from the trip, he

spent days debating if he should tell her so. "I just don't want her to shoot me down and never want to see me again," he'd say.

"That's fair," I'd reply. "But do you want to stay friends forever? Or do you want to find out if there's something really there?"

"Definitely not just friends," John would concede.

"Then you know what you gotta do," I'd coax him.

A few months later, John decided to tell Carly how he felt. After John spilled, she strung him along with statements like, "I really enjoy seeing you, John," and, "Our friendship means a lot to me, John." Then, after weeks of playing cat and mouse, Carly shared she was getting back together with her ex-boyfriend. Dagger.

For all the obvious reasons, John was beside himself. He was desperate to win Carly's affections so when Carly broke up (again) with her ex, he was there. He took her to her favorite restaurant. They played mini golf. They went to the mall. John stood by her, pursuing her.

The thing is, the more John chased love, the more he sabotaged himself. Carly not only learned to lean on him for emotional support when dealing with her baggage from other relationships, whenever John tried dating other women during time spent away from Carly, it never worked out. He compared everyone to some abstract, idealized "Carly."

I pulled over to a single-pump gas station and opened the tank to my car. As I watched the slow, methodical meter tick out a few gallons of fuel, I thought about one specific conversation I'd had with John. I had answered my phone to John mumbling in a slow, solemn voice. "Hey, dude," he said.

"John, what's up man? Where are you?" I inquired.

"Just driving," he said. "With a milkshake," he added after hesitating.

"Oh, cool," I replied, wondering where this was going. The way he paused made it sound like this particular dairy beverage was strapped into his passenger seat, as if it a companion, not something being consumed through a straw.

"What kind of milkshake?"

"Vanilla. Gas stations only have two flavors," John sighed.

I couldn't help but laugh. "Why are you drinking a gas station milkshake?"

"I was going to meet Carly to see a movie..." John started to explain before I cut him off.

"Bad idea man. Isn't she in grad school now? Hours away?"

"Yeah, she is, so I drove a few hours to meet her," he continued. "It was almost time for the show when I got there. I didn't see her so I called her, but she didn't answer except for a quick text to say 'I can't make it.' I didn't even get a sorry."

That was cold-blooded. "She's the worst," I offered. "You just have to forget her man..." I started to say before deciding it wasn't the right time to press the issue. "I'm really sorry, John. The milkshake was a good idea."

I'd grown so absorbed in reliving John's story that before I knew it, I was pulling into the community center I was scheduled to speak at. I stood outside and stretched my legs for a few minutes, thinking about the rest of John's story. After he finished that milkshake, he decided to give up the hunt. He stopped running after Carly. One year after that, we were at a wedding together and he met the girl he'd later marry. When he was no longer trying to discover love and he'd grown content with his relationship status, he finally found the love of his life.

―――

Jesus talked about this concept long before the days of Serta mattresses and gas-station milkshakes. Except he discussed it in the context of grace. He said we never catch grace if we chase it. He didn't just preach it, either. He lived it. He gave away grace so people stopped foraging for it.

Jesus lived, ate, and spoke with people seen as the milkshake-drinking rejects of their time. Abused widows, cultural cast-outs, and ashamed sinners who had no hope of climbing their society's ladder were the primary people he paid attention to. He promised them the forgiveness and healing they'd stopped striving for. *Go in peace. Your sins are forgiven. Your faith has healed you.* These were his words as he resolved the kinds of sickness and sins people spend fortunes on self-help books and seminars for.

Standing in stark contrast to Jesus' offer of unconditional grace were people called Pharisees. Pharisees weren't mythical creatures (although their name makes it sound like that's the case). They were the religious leaders of their day. They chased righteousness. They worked hard to follow the rules. They tried to live perfect lives. They didn't give handouts, and they made sure you bought all the books, at-home video sets, and tracked your progress in spreadsheets. However, it was the Pharisees' chase that prevented them from finding the very thing they sought – good standing with God.

While Jesus said people were free to have a relationship with God – they didn't have to earn it by trying really hard and following all the rules – the Pharisees scrutinized other people's lifestyles. Putting others down made them appear "holier than thou." It was the quickest way to the top of God's favorites list, or so they thought. Jesus described this when he said, "For [Pharisees] preach, but do not practice. They tie up heavy burdens, hard to bear, and lay them on people's shoulders, but they themselves are not willing to move them." (Matthew 23:3-5)

Ultimately, as they chased righteousness through their rules, rituals, and trying really hard, they ran right past the relationship Jesus was offering them.

I can't blame them too much, though. I honestly think I would have been one of them. I think the Pharisees liked the thrill of the chase. Grace feels too easy, otherwise. The idea, "For it's by grace you have been saved through faith. And this is not your own doing... so that no one may boast," (Ephesians 2:8-9) doesn't sound very attractive. It doesn't feel like grace is worth very much when we don't have to earn it.

Yet, grace is far from cheap. Jesus traded his life for it. Until we recognize the immense cost that was paid so we can receive grace unconditionally, we'll stay on our treadmill. Always running, never moving forward. By contrast, we'll reach the finish line and the ever-elusive sense of fulfillment from knowing we're enough, that we're loved, by doing nothing more than giving up the hustle.

As strange as it sounds when you're given a clear choice, to keep on striving or to stop the chase, it's often easier to keep pushing forward. I mean, how did you feel a week after buying your last smartphone? After your last promotion? Likely not as content as day one. So if you're like me, we fall right back into our chase and we forget Jesus' promise that, "[T]hose who drink the water I give will never be thirsty again. It becomes a fresh, bubbling spring within them, giving them eternal life." (John 4:14) Ending our chase with this water is far more filling than any gas station milkshake.

how to fly a hot air balloon

~ we only see light on our darkest days ~

Balloon rides mirror the human experience. Every day, we wake up to find our lives composed by two opposing forces. We find ourselves relying on warmth — kindness, love, compassion — to keep us afloat in the cold, cold surroundings of our world.

I didn't have much of a plan as I drove up to the two-terminal airfield in Southwest Colorado. Erin was flying in to meet me after my aforementioned road trip. We have family in that part of the state and my cousin was moving to Seattle, so my aunt and uncle had planned a farewell party. We'd join them for the party but beyond that, we had no set itinerary.

Erin hopped into my car and asked what I thought we'd do that weekend. "No clue," I shrugged. "I'm sure we'll find something."

As we ate dinner and watched the sun set over the neighboring San Juan Mountains later that evening, I asked my uncle for ideas.

"You know what?" He grinned before revealing a local secret. "It's Colorfest tomorrow. You'll love Colorfest."

"What's Colorfest?" We both asked.

"Balloonists from all around the country come to fly their hot air balloons. They launch them from a field near the river at sunrise. It's incredible. And out-of-town pilots often need volunteer crew."

"Which means," he continued, "If you show up early enough, you just might get to launch and fly in one of the balloons."

I slapped the table in excitement. I was sold. "We're doing that!"

I turned to Erin with an ear-to-ear grin. I was met with an expression that said something like, "No chance I'm riding in a wicker basket 2,000 feet above the ground without two years of safety training."

"Great idea! You'll have fun," my aunt added from the kitchen.

"What do you mean, 'show up early?' How do we know who the pilots are? Where do we get registered?" Erin quizzed my uncle on the finer details I'd bypassed while wondering what the world record for highest hot air balloon flight was (it's 69,850 feet, if you're curious).

"Oh, you know," he said casually. "Just show up at the park before sunrise and find the group of people huddled together. That's the pilot's briefing. The flight director talks about weather then so just walk in and ask around. Somebody will point you in the right direction."

"Here," he handed us a local newspaper. "There's the address."

"Done." I didn't need any convincing. "Whatcha think, Erin?"

"I guess we might as well give it a shot."

"Morning y'all!" The loudspeaker croaked as Erin and I walked into an oversized, carnival-style tent an hour before sunrise. "Get yourself biscuits, gravy, coffee, anythin' you need before we get goin'," a welcoming southern drawl instructed the group shuffling around in the dark.

"Biscuit?" I asked Erin.

"Definitely not. My stomach's nervous. Let's just figure out where the heck we check in," she said.

"I don't think there's a check in process," I chuckled. "I think we just ask people if they need help. You know, act like we're not completely new at this."

"But we are new at this," Erin reminded me. "We stick out like sore thumbs." She pointed to the matching jackets everyone except us were sporting. "Just look at that guy. He's got wings clipped to his jacket and a buzzcut. He's legit."

After the pilots briefing concluded a few minutes later, we made our way to the front of the tent and heard someone shout, "Crew? Volunteers? Anyone?"

"Yes!" My hand shot up. "Us!" I yelled out and pulled Erin toward the voice.

"Okay! Over here," the voice directed us toward a group of four crew members in matching jackets.

"We'll take'em," the crew chief, Katie, confirmed.

We shook hands and followed Katie to a pickup truck with a bed full of balloon parts. An industrial fan, a wicker basket, a nylon canopy, fuel tanks, the works. We piled into the truck and drove a few minutes to the launch site as Katie laid out the ground rules.

"I'm your crew chief today. That means whatever I say goes. Alright? You do what I say, and don't do anything I don't say, even if you think it's right. Balloons are licensed aircraft, so we follow a certain process to ensure we always fly safely. Got it?"

Katie had served as a helicopter mechanic in the Air Force for a decade so she knew her stuff. Erin, queen of all things safety, listened intently.

"Once the envelope's rolled out, we'll check the panels, skirt, tethers, then get the basket hooked up. Sound good?"

We nodded, not totally sure what she had said. "Envelope" turned out to be the official word for the colored balloon. In any event, twenty minutes later, our pilot, Mike, began pumping hot air from the burners into it. I stood back and watched, wide-eyed. It grew like a king cobra rising up from its coil. After the purple, yellow, and green canopy rose to its peak height, it towered more than 100 feet overhead. It was impressive, to say the least. I had no idea hot air balloons are taller than most office buildings.

Mike made sure his flight instruments were in working order and Katie handed us a pen and paper. "Want to go for a ride? Just sign these release forms and Mike will take you up."

Flying in a hot air balloon was very different from what I was expecting. It was quieter than an airplane, steadier than a glider, and more calming than thrilling. As we climbed higher and higher, I understood why the festival had been dubbed "Colorfest." Every color of the rainbow was represented in a perfect, 360-degree panorama. Yellow aspens and green, purple, and blue balloons were scattered across a canvas of an orange-red sunrise. It was the kind of beauty that makes you wiggle, like your mind can't process all the splendor so it spills over and makes your legs and arms quiver.

"This is spectacular," I whispered to Erin. She beamed as she clenched the wicker basket.

"I don't think we'll forget this," she whispered back.

"So, this is why you fly in the mornings, huh?" I said to Mike as he opened the burner to climb again. "To see the sunrise?"

"Not exactly," Mike replied.

"Sunrises are nice, but it's so our balloons fly better. Hot air only creates lift when the air inside the balloon is *much* hotter than the air outside it. The contrast in temperature is what gets us to lift off, and first light is always the coldest part of the day."

I stared into the massive, radiant dome floating above my head. I thought about how our balloon worked. We spend so much of our weeks directing motion. Planes, cars, trains, bikes. They take us where we want to go, when we want to go. But balloons don't actually "go" anywhere – there's no way to steer them. There's just one route, up and down. There are no rudders nor propulsion to help you navigate so your direction is determined by the wind, and descending is done by letting air out of the balloon; as the hot air drains, the temperature inside nears the temperature outside and you sink.

We floated for a few more minutes, silently taking in the scene and pretending there was no basket below our feet before Mike interrupted. "Time to put her down," he said. "Look for fences and powerlines, will you? Shout 'em out, even if you think I see 'em."

"Can do!" Erin spoke up.

As we looked for power lines, I noticed a bright orange flag tracing our flight. It was Katie in the pickup truck. She was tailing the balloon's path, ready to haul the rig back to town and refill the fuel tanks for us. "Okay Katie," Mike radioed. "Looks like we'll put down next to that barn, 'bout a mile south from you."

That seemed funny to me. Someone could be eating pancakes at their kitchen table one moment, and the next, they'd watch a 100-foot balloon drop into their backyard. That's how it had to work, though. We were running low on fuel and we couldn't direct our flight, so we'd land wherever the wind said we would.

I think balloon rides mirror the human experience. Every day, we arise to find our lives composed by two opposing forces. We rely on warmth — kindness, love, compassion — to stay afloat in the cold surroundings of a world struggling to overcome death, grief, and depression. This past week, a friend who'd worked training nonprofit leaders for fifteen years was laid off from his job (and health benefits) and diagnosed with cancer in the same week. When these kinds of cold headwinds threaten to collapse us, we try to fill our days back up with warm things like laughter, celebration, and joy (I brought him a big chocolate cake).

The Bible's authors write about the contrast between cold and warm, good and bad, all throughout the text. Whether it's subtle, like Jesus whispering, "Father, forgive them, for they do not know what they are doing," (Luke 23:24) as he's bloodied and dying, or more direct, like John writing, "In him was life, and that life was the light of all mankind. The light shines in the darkness, and the darkness has not overcome it." (John 1:4-5) Each of the writers denotes a clear and immutable separation between light, which represents good, and dark, which represents evil.

The point that a difference between these categories exists may not seem strange to you at first. It probably sounds obvious, in fact. Evil is not good, and good is not evil. Light is not dark, and dark is not light. We know this, and we believe dark and evil, tragedy and heartbreak, should have no place in our world. But in the context of our modern ethics, this is now a very strange thing to say. It cuts against the relative morality glorified in our culture.

Today, there is no clear divide between good and bad, light and dark. It's left to the individual to define according to their own feelings and preferences. Someone's "truth" may not be another's. We're not allowed to make absolute statements like, "Sex before marriage is bad," or, "You shouldn't cuss just because you're angry." *Says who?* is the response. The problem with this approach to morality is the contrast between absolutes is actually a helpful and supportive part of the human experience for two reasons.

The first is relatively straightforward; we can only truly see light because of our darkest days. Contrast gives us an appreciation for the gifts we have. For example, salty pepperoni pizza never tastes better than after a marathon. It's the struggle to pound out all those sweat-filled miles that turns normal, everyday pizza into a slice of heaven. Contrast helps us know when we're flying high in life.

The second reason is that the distinction between good and evil signals the existence of something far greater than the opposites. When we have some type of abject, visceral reaction to evil, like cancer and unemployment, we're appealing to some objective basis upon which we say people *should* be healthy and employed. We're differentiating what's good and what's evil by a third thing outside the two which makes us feel, "That's just not right!" That's because what we use to measure an item and the item itself can't be one in the same. There's a separate and external point of reference.

This is very important because when we measure something physical, like an inseam, a measuring tape gets the job done. But when we're attempting to measure morality and degrees of good and evil, a physical device won't cut it. Our point of reference must reside in the spiritual realm, and this provides an incredible opportunity for us to stick out in today's culture. One of history's greatest authors on this topic, C.S. Lewis, says:

> *My argument against God was that the universe seemed so cruel and unjust. But how had I got this idea of just and unjust? A man does not call a line crooked unless he has some idea of a straight line. What was I comparing this universe with when I called it unjust?* [11]

No doubt, we all feel our world is not as it should be. Bad things shouldn't happen to good people. So, it's natural to feel God can't exist if our world has spiraled out of control. But as Lewis says, we can only know things are amiss because someone transcendent, far above and outside us, said there's a difference between good and evil.

We couldn't have arrived at this conclusion by ourselves:

> *If the whole universe has no meaning, we should never have found out that it has no meaning: just as, if there were no light in the universe and therefore no creatures with eyes, we should never know it was dark. Dark would be without meaning.*[12]

In the world of hot air balloons, we have thermometers to tell us the difference in air temperature. In our world, someone gave us a compass – a conscience – to navigate the difference. But, as our hot air balloon ride reminded me, the instruments we use to discern if we're on or off course can't also put us back on course. Instruments don't stop us from crashing back to earth when we run out of fuel. They only tell us there's a problem. We need a savior to lift us up when we run out of fuel and the cold, dark things of the world threaten to overwhelm us. To return to Lewis' perspective:

> *God made us: invented us as a man invents an engine. A car is made to run on petrol, and it would not run properly on anything else. Now God designed the human machine to run on Himself. He Himself is the fuel our spirits were designed to burn, or the food our spirits were designed to feed on. There is no other. That is why it is just no good asking God to make us happy in our own way without bothering about religion. God cannot give us a happiness and peace apart from Himself, because it is not there.*[13]

We depend on God to get us back on course and fill up our lives with happiness, warmth, and joy when we've run low. But this raises an age-old question, doesn't it? *If God is good, why does He allow evil? Besides, why would we even desire a relationship with a god that allows evil?* Stephen Fry, the English writer, actor, and activist articulated this when he was asked what he'd say to God if they were to meet face-to-face:

> *How dare you? How dare you create a world to which there is such misery that is not our fault. It's not right, it's utterly, utterly evil. Why should I respect a capricious, mean-minded, stupid God who creates a world that is so full of injustice and pain? That's what I would say.*[14]

If Mr. Lewis were to respond to Mr. Fry, he may have said:

> *God created things which had free will. That means creatures which can go wrong or right. Some people think they can imagine a creature which was free but had no possibility of going wrong, but I can't. If a thing is free to be good it's also free to be bad. And free will is what has made evil possible. Why, then, did God give them free will? Because free will, though it makes evil possible, is also the only thing that makes possible any love or goodness or joy worth having. A world of automata – of creatures that worked like machines – would hardly be worth creating. The happiness which God designs for His higher creatures is the happiness of being freely, voluntarily united to Him and to each other in an ecstasy of love and delight compared with which the most rapturous love between a man and a woman on this earth is mere milk and water. And for that they've got to be free. Of course, God knew what would happen if they used their freedom the wrong way: apparently, He thought it worth the risk... If God thinks this state of war in the universe a price worth paying for free will – that is, for making a real world in which creatures can do real good or*

> *harm and something of real importance can happen, instead of a toy world which only moves when He pulls the strings – then we may take it it is worth paying.*[15]

Mr. Fry is right in that the onslaught of headlines featuring refugees, racism, and rape don't seem just. Every day, there's an undeniable and ostensible presence of evil in our world. But as Lewis reminds us, there is also good, which points to an authority greater than us. And as John's gospel reminds us, that authority is sovereign. *The light shines in the darkness, and the darkness has not overcome it.*

So in a world that's lost the contrast between right and wrong, good and evil, let's stick out by committing to living as Jesus did. Let's chase down friends who've depleted their fuel tanks and are plunging toward a crash landing. Let's confront the cold things in our neighbors' lives with glowing compassion. And when we live good, warm lives in contrast to an evil, cold world, I believe others will begin to see the light during their darkest days.

climbing gray's in a whiteout

~ difficult experiences are the hardest to forget ~
If we choose to follow Jesus, we'll be called into the whiteout, often feeling like we're sliding on our butts down frozen rocks. Rarely will we be equipped for what we'll encounter.

Coloradans climb 14ers like New Yorkers eat bagels. There are a lot of varieties to try, and you're not really a native unless you're able to list the mountains/delis you frequent. Coloradans, however, believe summiting 14ers is much cooler than eating bagels, and deli sandwiches for that manner. (For the uninitiated, a 14er is a mountain whose peak rises higher than 14,000 feet in elevation.)

You've likely noticed some patterns in my stories at this point, so you can probably sense this is one cult tradition I can get behind. I love adventure, the outdoors, and a good challenge. Putting them all together in the form of a statewide ritual feels like the greatest hobby ever.

The first time Erin and I summited a 14er is a moment I'll never forget, but it's an experience she really would like to. We were totally unprepared for what unfolded during our ascent, and while that only heightened the sense of adventure in my mind, it was so distressing to Erin she wouldn't entertain the thought of climbing another 14er for quite some time.

Generally, we believe we create memories with our minds, but as we previously discussed, it's our emotions that determine what we retain. We don't actually see memories for what they are. Feelings are sticky, and they attach themselves to past events as we construct memories based upon what we felt in the moment. When we recall past events, the facts may be fuzzy, but the sensations are as sharp as ever – especially the negative ones.

When I think about this particular trek up a 14er called Gray's, I don't remember how many switchbacks we navigated or how many miles we hiked. I can only vaguely recall the feeling of standing on the summit. Erin, on the other hand, remembers with scrupulous detail how miserable she felt while sliding down ice-covered scree, wishing our day would come to an early end. There's a reason for that – it's the painful memories we'd most like to forget that are toughest to leave behind.

———

I squeezed my watch as its glowing face said it was time to rise and shine. It was a few hours before sunrise, but we needed to break down our campsite near the base of Gray's Peak and get moving. Mountain weather becomes increasingly variable in the afternoon, so we'd have to start our descent down the face far before then. I folded our tent and crammed my sleeping bag into its stuff-sack. Once our gear was neatly consolidated, I sat down beside Erin and gratefully accepted a cup of coffee.

"How'd y'all sleep?" One of our friends, Grant, called. He was standing next to his wife, Bre, and our other friend, Danny, who had shared their tent that night. They had their packs and headlamps strapped on, ready to start our journey.

"Just fine," I said. "You guys?"

"Well..." Danny sighed. "Bre woke up in a midnight stupor, shouting that someone was trying to get into our tent. Freaked me out! I didn't sleep much after that."

"Bummer." I laughed as I studied Danny's bare legs. "Shorts? You going to be warm enough in those?"

"Yeah man, we Peruvians are cold weather people," he chuckled. "Besides, it's supposed to be pretty sunny today."

"Hope so," I nodded.

"You guys ready to roll?" Grant, the native Coloradan among us, asked. "We should head out if we want to make both Gray's and Torrey's," he advised, referring to Gray's sister peak, which you can reach by traversing a saddle connecting the two summits.

Our journey began as we navigated a skinny trail cut through thick sagebrush. I turned around to watch the dispersed trail of headlamps tracing our footsteps every so often. The track of lights from other hikers looked like little ants following breadcrumbs we'd dropped along the path. As the sun gently rose a few hours later, we all stopped to suck down some water.

"So far so easy," I said as I attacked a granola bar and gazed up at the looming rock walls on either side of the valley.

"I think I'm a little too hydrated," Erin spoke up. "I'm going to find somewhere to do my thing."

A few minutes later, Erin came running back to our group. "Did you guys know there's a huge cliff that way? Like, sheer, hundred-foot-drop-off huge. I was almost toast!"

"Okay, we'll stick together now," I reassured her. "No worries."

Shortly after we resumed our trek, the temperature began to plummet. Normally, the temperature climbs as the rising Colorado sun shines. On this particular morning, however, it was getting so cold that if we stopped moving, we began to shiver and rub our hands together to generate heat. We were all wearing some sort of light windbreaker, but none of us had planned for winter weather.

"Graupel, that's interesting," Grant said as he swiped his hand along a rock, inspecting the wintry mix clinging to his glove.

"You nerd," Bre joked, referring to Grant's weather science master's degree.

"Well this *graupel* is making my hands as cold as Danny's legs. Let's get moving again," Erin said.

We kept moving up the trail and slowly but surely we started to see hikers in front of us turning around. It was either too snowy, slick, or just plain miserable to continue. In fact, the wind smacking my hood was so loud I couldn't hear Erin expressing how much the weather sucked until she was close enough to tap me.

After another hour of moving up the trail, we were closing in on the summit. Roughly 600 feet of vertical elevation remained between us and the finish line when we crouched down out of the wind to assess everyone's status. Erin was miserable. Danny didn't look too good. The altitude was getting to him, and he was a little queasy. Grant and Bre, like me, were cold, but up to make a final push to the peak.

The deceptive part about summiting a 14er is the thin air. As you gain elevation, it compounds the effort of each additional step. Hiking at one mile high is one thing, hiking 9,000 feet above that is a different experience. The blowing, wintry mix quickly turned to snow as Erin shivered in her windbreaker.

Less than an hour later, we all made the summit. Shaking from the cold and winded from the effort, we held up a sign that read "GRAYS PEAK, 14,278FT" and posed for a picture. There were no breathtaking views, no gazing across the Rockies from atop the world.

Instead, we stood in front of a solid white backdrop. I kid you not, apart from the earth-colored rocks around our feet, the rest of that photo is as pure white as a brand-new bedsheet. We were standing on the peak of a 14er in the middle of a pure whiteout, and clearly, we hadn't come prepared.

"I can't even see Torrey's," I said to Grant after we snapped a few photos. "This is going to get sketchy."

"Yeah, there's zero visibility," Grant agreed.

"We're not considering hiking across, right?" Erin overhead us.

"Well, we should get Danny to lower elevation," I pointed out.

Grant nodded. "No doubt. I'm amazed he made it up here."

We all agreed traversing to Torrey's Peak was too risky. It would be just as risky to split the group, so it was settled. We'd all head down after spending just a few minutes atop Gray's. As we picked our way down the slope, I considered how people always talk about making it to the top of a mountain. Really, we should talk more about making it down.

The trek down Gray's was just as exhausting and more mentally taxing than the hike up. The once light and fluffy snow turned to ice and created a slick, glassy film on every surface we grabbed or stepped on. The unstable footing and gravity's unforgiving force conspired to bring us crashing onto the jagged rock time and time again.

Eventually, we made it off the mountainside. When we passed the valley and reached the trailhead, I knew we'd never forget that trip, no matter how many mountains we visited. Erin, however, was convinced she'd never hike another 14er. She preferred to forget the experience altogether.

If you were to ask about that trip up Gray's, I would say it was incredible, while Erin would say it was incredibly unenjoyable. Erin recalls feeling such intense discomfort that her impression of 14ers was colored with a dark shade for quite some time.

For a while, I'd joke about picking more, and more difficult, peaks to climb, just to get a rise out of her. I'd always get a reaction because as far as she was concerned, she was done with 14ers. Nevertheless, whenever I'd mention hiking Gray's in a whiteout, she couldn't help but recall our experience in *vivid* detail. The feelings of whipping wind and sliding down icy rocks still rush to her mind.

We all have memories we label as either pleasurable or painful. Strangely, it's the painful times we most want to forget that are most deeply ingrained into our brains. They seem to find the folder marked *Do Not Erase*. Even a years-old event can feel as fresh and raw as an event that occurred yesterday. It's why Erin reacts so strongly to the mention of 14ers.

Pleasurable moments, by contrast, usually fade with time. It's easier for the details of euphoric experiences – like summiting Gray's, from my perspective – to escape us. They're written over by more recent experiences, as if the folder labeled *Keep* in our brains hit its storage limit.

A Boston-based psychologist, Elizabeth Kensinger, backed this phenomenon with evidence in a groundbreaking study.[16] She found people who feel negative emotions during an event are far more likely to accurately recount the event. Similarly, she discovered we retain adverse memories for far longer than pleasurable ones. A plausible explanation is that threatening times are more valuable to our brains; they help us survive and avoid future pain.

That seems reasonable. However, I think there are other factors at work here too. Personally, I tend to internalize my flaws while writing off my accomplishments as accidents. I attribute wins as good things that just happened to go my way, while I hold myself personally accountable for my failures. "If only I had just..." is the start of too many sentences in my life. I know holding onto screw-ups and painful experiences is no way to live. If I always allow the sweet moments that lighten the sting of past pains to fade away, it's only a matter of time before I'll be crushed under a mounting burden of years-worth of negative memories.

Luckily, Jesus has a better way of life. He showed us it's possible to live lightly in a world filled with heavy, grievous moments. While life will never consist of four-hour lunch breaks and weekly salary bonuses, he said that's more than okay. In fact, he regularly sent his followers into the whiteout.

The twelve disciples who followed Jesus were called to face down some pretty serious stuff like diseases and demons. I've never seen a demon, but I have to imagine they're not pretty. The sight probably sticks in your mind for quite some time. Yet, as they left to tackle the dark side of our world, Jesus instructed, "Take nothing for your journey, no staff, nor bag, nor bread, nor money; and do not have two tunics." (Luke 9:1-3) He didn't even allow a windbreaker.

This call isn't unique to these twelve men. If we choose to truly follow Jesus, we too will be called into the unknown, and often feel like we're sliding on our butts down frozen rocks. Rarely will we be equipped for what we'll encounter.

This seems counterproductive on the surface, like Jesus just doesn't know how to read a weather forecast. I think it's all for our good, however. I think Jesus wants us to follow the path he's created, instead of making our own way and wandering off the side of a mountain. Faithfully following Jesus into the whiteout will always be hard work, but fortunately, he'll guide us along the way. When our past produces feelings of guilt, anger, and sadness, he cloaks us in grace, forgiveness, and hope to keep us moving forward. He reminds us that he's already walked the hard road to Calvary, and that "no one comes to the Father except through me." (John 14:6)

Even the apostle Paul, a man whose past was stained with the memories of executing Jesus' followers in the bloodiest of ways, was able to write, "[I]f anyone is in Christ, he is a new creation. The old has passed away; behold, the new has come." (2 Cor. 5:17) Paul didn't cling to the oppressive experiences he'd rather forget, saying to himself, "If only I'd killed one less Christian…" He embraced the joy and new life he found while following Jesus' call.

A French priest and professor, Henri Nouwen, wrote about this intersection between mental health and spirituality. Some of his most salient words read:

> *To be grateful for the good things that happen in our lives is easy, but to be grateful for all of our lives, the good as well as the bad, the moments of joy as well as the moments of sorrow, the successes as well as the failures, the rewards as well as the rejections, that requires hard spiritual work. Still, we are only grateful people when we can say thank you to all that has brought us to the present moment. As long as we keep dividing our lives between events and people we would like to remember and those we would rather forget, we cannot claim the fullness of our beings as a gift of God to be grateful for. Let's not be afraid to look at everything that has brought us to where we are now and trust that we will soon see in it the guiding hand of a loving God.*[17]

Everyone embraces the wins and warm moments. Standing on a mountain top in the sunshine is the easy part. Enduring whiteouts and leg-burning trials while unprepared is the challenge that sticks with us long-term. I think, though, that's exactly why Mr. Nouwen says we're to be grateful for both kinds of experiences. God uses both pleasure and pain to shape us for his glory and our good.

a blind haircut

~ we learn more with less information ~
By funneling the entirety of the Jewish law into two sentences, Jesus beat the test and broke the chains shackling his culture.

———————

Let's face it. Most of the news, photos, and content we consume is a waste. We live in a noisy world, so media is sensationalized to break through to us. It has to be; we've grown weary from information overload. Our brains are struggling to sift what's important from what's not. We see 3,000 corporate logos every single day. We read news from eight separate sources, on average. Our attention spans have disintegrated and are now, in fact, shorter than a goldfish's.[18] It's no wonder we've grown anesthetized to everything but headlines and highlights.

This presents a considerable challenge for us because not everything that shocks us brings us life. Not everything sensational is also meaningful. If we wish to live meaningful lives, we have to strip away all this stimulus. While it sounds a little strange, the more we dial back the flow of information, the more we're able to absorb. That's the paradox of our five senses. As you remove one sense, the others grow exponentially more sensitive.

This matters because life will always bring us hardship. When we inevitably find ourselves facing down conflict, whether it be unemployment, the death of a friend, depression, guilt, obesity, a breakup, or what have you, those who live shallow lives will be washed away. But if we've taken the time to soak up life, have rich conversations, and move beyond superficial exchanges, we'll find ourselves grounded amidst life's adversity.

For example, a few years ago, a massive storm rolled through Western England and Northern Ireland.[19] This region is very rainy, so the topsoil is always saturated and trees can find the nutrients they need without growing deep roots. These trees live at a surface level. Typically, storms snap a tree's limbs while its roots anchor it to the earth. But in this particular storm, acres upon acres of trees were entirely uprooted. Can you imagine that? Generations-worth of trees were *completely* toppled and forest preserves, public spaces, and family estates went bald.

In today's age of misinformation, social media, and "alternative facts" designed to align our minds with certain political parties, products, and lifestyles, it's worth noting we're on an eerily similar trajectory. Like the United Kingdom's trees, we're at risk of living off surface-level nutrients. We're media-saturated and we rarely take the time to cultivate the kinds of deep roots that can sustain us during life's storms.

So how do we move beyond shallow exchanges and live deeply? With a wealth of information but a poverty of attention placed on the topics that truly matter, where do we begin? While there are many answers, a blind child visiting a barbershop showed me where we might start.

I peered past my *Entrepreneur* magazine and noticed a slender black pole sitting in the middle of the walkway. I was sitting in a row of seats at the front of the barbershop, patiently waiting my turn. *Someone's going to trip over that thing,* I thought to myself.

As I looked around to determine why a tripping hazard had been left in the middle of everyone's footpath, I realized that narrow stick was actually meant to *prevent* someone from tripping. A child wearing sunglasses and a crooked smile gripped the pole's leather-bound handle. He seemed to be eight, maybe nine years old. He gazed wistfully in the direction of a small bell that signaled another patron's entrance. If his sunglasses and stick hadn't given it away, his aimless gazing toward the shop's various noises confirmed it; he was blind.

"James?" A stylist called out from the back of the barbershop.

Evidently, his name was James, as he sprang up from his chair. His mother leaned his stick against the wall and guided him to an old fashioned, black leather barber's chair. She conferred with the stylist for a moment, sharing James liked his hair short on top, but not so short that he wouldn't be able to run his fingers through it.

The stylist nodded and fired up her clippers. She brought them near James' ear and he winced as they touched his head, recoiling from the loud mechanical noise. His nose wrinkled and his brow furrowed as the stylist moved the shears toward his neck. As I watched, it occurred to me James likely relied on sounds to determine what's friendly and what's not. It was a curious thing. He was so incredibly sensitive to everything around him. On several occasions, the stylist had to redirect his head to face forward as he wiggled around, turning toward the shop's sounds.

I realized I was staring after another minute. I wanted to be observant without being offensive, so I glanced over to his mother. She'd picked up a book and appeared to be focused on the pages, so I continued to watch James. The stylist grabbed a pair of scissors and started trimming the top of his sandy blonde hair. Without the white noise of the clippers drowning out the din of the barbershop, James seemed even more interested in what was happening around him. He craned his neck toward every jingle and clanking noise, and the stylist continued to reposition him. I imagined James was using the cacophony to construct a scene as vivid and as detailed as anything I was watching.

Once she finished, the stylist leaned against a silver lever and reclined the overstuffed chair towards a sink. James smiled the kind of wide, open-mouth smile you'd expect to see from a kid riding a rollercoaster. His face lit up with delight as sudsy hands and pressurized water massaged his scalp. After a towel dry, comb, and some gel, James stood up from the chair looking like a new man. He beamed as his mom told him how nice he looked.

Will I have that much fun getting my hair cut today? I wondered.

Generally speaking, I love going to the barber. There's a unique, brand-new feeling the barber gives you. But this particular trip felt more like a chore. I'd been sitting far longer than my predicted wait time. A longer wait meant a later finish, which meant I'd have less time to finish replacing the kitchen faucet I'd been tinkering with. In turn, that meant I wouldn't start cooking dinner until I was already hungry, which meant I'd be a grouch... you get the idea.

These were all trivial concerns in the grand scheme of things. Nevertheless, as I oscillated between emailing on my phone, watching ESPN on the TV, and reading my *Entrepreneur* magazine in a sad attempt to medicate my impatience, I grew increasingly restless. Just listening to the sounds of the shop and reflecting on my week didn't feel like productive ways to spend my time. I just wanted to check 'haircut' off my list and move on with my week.

James' mother handed the stylist a cash tip as they strolled toward the storefront. As they walked, it occurred to me that James was leading her, dragging his walking stick behind them. He grabbed the door handle and once outside, he walked toward his mother's vehicle, stopping in front of the passenger door to wait for the chime signaling that the door had been unlocked. Clearly, James had studied his steps. He remembered the layout of the shop and parking lot, so he was able to retrace his path without aid.

As I pocketed my phone and set my magazine in its rack, I had to laugh. I'm always rushing through my weeks without stopping to learn from them. I'm running from place to place, distracted by the focus of the day. If I could somehow get back all the hours I've spent repeating the same mistakes I've already made and should have moved past, I'd have a year of free time. Easy.

This day was no exception. I was in a rush to leave the barbershop and get on with life. I wasn't interested in unplanned downtime and extra waiting. Shuffling through my barrage of email and obsessing over my too-tight schedule was far easier than spending a few moments contemplating my week. James, on the other hand, clearly took his time navigating his weeks. He soaked up his surroundings despite his lack of sight, which helped him find his way around.

Back in your school days, did you ever cram for an exam? You know, where you'd shove 100 pages worth of information into your brain in less than two minutes? If so, I'll bet you don't remember any of those facts or figures. Everyone knew the trick was to finish cramming right before the professor handed out the exam because all that knowledge would start leaking from your ears right after.

My life often feels like one constant test I'm cramming for. You could chalk that up to my over-achieving personality, but I seem to find myself with a progressively demanding schedule and crowded calendar every year I'm on this earth. Though I've tried to shortcut my way through various tests, cramming only ever serves to back me into a corner. Living well has required that I move beyond shortcuts and adopt new rhythms and routines into my week, like reading Psalms before reaching for my phone, writing before I turn on a movie, and praying before I close my eyes at night.

Jesus challenged his followers to do exactly this. To live deeply and think critically. At the time, rote memorization of as many religious laws and guidelines as humanly possible was the cultural norm. The Pharisees, among the time's most prominent influencers, forced people to memorize all 613 Jewish commandments. They were legalistic, highly religious, and they were ruthless.

One day, a member of the Pharisee's leading ranks decided he'd go toe-to-toe with Jesus. He was a lawyer, exceptionally trained in both recalling the law's fine print and examining others, so he put Jesus to the test. He asked Jesus, "Teacher, which is the greatest commandment in the Law?" (Matthew 22:35-36) But this question was more than a test. It was a trap. If Jesus selected just one of the 613 laws, that left 612 opportunities for the lawyer to say he was wrong. But if Jesus refused to provide an answer, he'd be portrayed as foolish, uncertain of the law, and unfit to teach his followers.

Little did this lawyer know Jesus was not only smarter than the Pharisees' schemes, he took a simpler approach to defining a well-lived life. He freed his followers from the tyranny of the law and upheld it in the same breath. He distilled an entire culture which drowned people in hundreds of traditions and rituals into just two short sentences by replying, "You shall love the Lord your God with all your heart and with all your soul and with all your mind. This is the great and first commandment. And a second is like it: You shall love your neighbor as yourself. On these two commandments depend all the Law and the Prophets." (Matthew 22:37-40)

By funneling the entirety of Jewish law into two sentences, Jesus beat the test and broke the chains shackling his culture. Not so different from today, the Pharisees' way of life overwhelmed people with information. There was always a new interpretation, a new emphasis on certain ways of life, so people scrambled to keep up, learn from their teachers, and apply all 613 laws. By contrast, Jesus' two-sentence approach trained his disciples for the most important mission ever in just three years. He showed his followers how to build churches and transform broken communities in less time than it takes to earn a college degree.

It seems strange in a world of always-on news and access-anywhere updates, but by slowing down the flow of information we're able to soak in more of what matters. By shutting off one of our senses – practically speaking, that could look like praying in silence, listening to a sermon in the dark (it works), or singing praise acapella – it becomes easier to receive what the Lord wants to teach us. The proof is when life's storms come, and just like James who found his way out of the barbershop without his cane, we're able to navigate our way home.

sorry, not this year

~bring out the best in others to reveal the best in you~
Just like the sea sitting below the streams around it, increasing in power and grandeur as the earth's rivers are drawn toward it, we also gravitate toward those who lower themselves. By pointing out the best in others, by extension, you reveal the best in you.

Belle, the chocolate lab we adopted, loves praise. She loves belly rubs too, but she'll do anything so long as you tell her she's a good girl. She'll even walk around the house picking up her toys if you tell her how proud you are. She's not bashful about seeking your praise, either. She'll look at you with her brown eyes and a titled expression wondering, "Am I a good girl today?"

Belle and I aren't so different. Honestly, I might crave praise more than her. I may not wriggle my rear-end in excitement when someone says, "Good job, Nate!" but my ego is definitely more fragile. Belle just needs a walk and a treat as a reward, I need more consistent affirmation.

While it's unsurprising my emotions are more complex than a canine's, I don't think I'm unique. I think we all live to hear the words, "Well done." We long for the inner peace of knowing we're enough, that we measure up in the eyes of others. To borrow Dale Carnegie's words, "I can look back at my own life and see where a few words of praise have sharply changed my entire future. Can't you say the same thing about your life?"[20]

In our pursuit of praise, we typically elevate our good qualities and shove the negatives one into the junk drawer that hides all our dead batteries, coupons, and rubber bands. For example, I make sure my co-workers see my ambition. I never disclose the moments in which it limits the time I spend with family. That typically works for a while, but a self-promoting, image-managing approach to securing others' approval isn't sustainable. It's ugly.

The pop culture columns in the Washington Post and New York Times recently featured our new alternative to boasting – the "humblebrag."[21] That's using fake humility to make declaring your awesomeness a little more palatable. For example, if you're to say, "I can't stand flying first class. I have to sit on the plane longer than everyone before we take off." Or, "It's so hard being the company's smartest employee. Everyone asks me to stay late and help them with their projects," that's humblebragging.

But if boasting is ugly, the humblebrag is insincere, and our craving for adoration remains unquenched, where can we turn? Who will validate us?

While it seems to run counter to the question, I believe we'll do best by lifting others up. By placing someone else above ourselves, we demonstrate our capacity for humility and modesty. These are far nobler, more attractive characteristics. Besides, if we all desire praise and we need the occasional, "You're doing a great job," don't others want to live with people who make them feel valued too? Like the sea that sits below the streams around it, increasing in power and grandeur as the earth's rivers are drawn toward it, we gravitate toward those who lower themselves. By pointing out the best in others, by extension, you reveal the best in you.

We all have a certain "ness" about us. I have a Nate-ness to me. You have a you-ness to you. Before we discover our ness, we're impressionable. As we search for what makes us special, our sense of identity, we need someone to point us in the right direction. We need a guide who's willing to use their words to bring out the best in us and equip us for the journey ahead.

Personally, I was never more sensitive to the words of those around me than during my high school years. I clung to feedback from my teachers, peers, and especially the girls I liked. Naturally, I wasn't sure who I was becoming during these years. For better or worse, I looked to others' input to define me. Fortunately, this was the same time in which I met my high school baseball coach, Willie. When I met Willie, I immediately knew I wanted to be known as a person who did things the right way. I wanted to work hard and demonstrate integrity.

I previously wrote that during my freshman year, I was one of two students below five feet tall. The other guy, Dave, didn't care for baseball, so I was the one runt trying to prove he could help the team's dream of winning a state title. My diminutive stature meant I couldn't hit the ball out of the infield. I was slow rounding the bases. I didn't have the reach to stop hard-hit balls from squirting into the outfield. In short, I left a lot to be desired. I did have one thing going for me, however. I had a fire in my belly. I was determined to prove I'd be more motivated than any other player.

That approach worked. Willie knew baseball was about life, not some state title that didn't matter too much anyway. He was in the business of training men as much as ball players so on the first day I walked onto Willie's baseball field, he told me to straighten my hat and tuck in my shirt. He was always talking about "discipline," and conducting ourselves well. We did things the right way or not at all. He didn't tolerate shortcuts, like showing up to gameday with dirty cleats. Willie had more experience than every coach in the state so we listened to him.

When we'd drive the team bus to away games, Willie wouldn't leave until I was sitting in the passenger's seat. He was a scout for the San Diego Padres, so I'd listen to him talk on the phone about big-league stuff as we drove. After he'd hang up, he'd fill me in on what really happens behind the scenes in the major leagues. The combination of sitting up front and listening to the pros talk shop said I had a place on Willie's team, regardless of my ability to crush doubles and chase ground balls.

When Willie looked at me sitting in the passenger seat chewing sunflower seeds, I think he saw a wide-eyed kid trying to make himself into something through sheer effort. I also think he knew the baseball field made me pliable; I'd listen and apply what he taught me. I'm sure that's why he gave me a jersey, because it certainly wasn't my athletic prowess.

When Willie told me I would be a ball player on his team, what I really heard him say was, "You're enough. Come belong here." I appreciated that more than he knew. When my junior year rolled around, Willie started coaching the varsity team. Playing for him with a varsity letter was going to be the peak of my high school career, maybe even my life. I was beyond excited, and I put in my best effort during the two-day tryouts, like I always had. Except this time, it wasn't enough.

Willie called me into his office right after tryouts. As I walked in, I was all smiles. I figured we were going to talk about the new uniforms, the away game schedule, or something you'd discuss with the guy who rode in your passenger seat. When Willie didn't say anything, I started to grow concerned. Then, tears began to slip down his cheeks.

He just shook his head and whispered, "Not this year, Nate. I'm so sorry. Not this year."

I started to cry too, but I quickly choked back my sobs. I wanted Willie to know that I'd learned how to be a man. That I'd grown up and could remember to tuck in my shirt on my own. As sad as I felt, I was thankful for Willie's tears. Strangely, they told me the baseball field didn't define who I was. His sniffles confirmed our relationship wasn't merely transactional, that my worth wasn't limited to my utility as a position player.

As I walked out of his office, Willie said I'd always be one of his favorite players. He told me I was becoming someone he was proud of, no matter what the roster said. You see, Willie knew people typically turn out the way we say they will. If we tell them they're loved, they'll act like loveable people. Willie gave me a sense of dignity to live out, and for that, he'll always be a giant in my memory.

Jesus was in the business of shaping lives too. He regularly picked people who looked like they'd be as much help as a short kid on a baseball field, and he used them to change the world. He once told a bunch of guys on a boat, "I will make you fishers of men," and with those few words, he gave them a higher calling. (Matthew 4:19) He didn't talk to them as insignificant laborers who, I'm sure, smelled pretty nasty. He turned them into students of a renowned teacher.

Jesus let them listen to big-league conversations in the passenger seat. He let them into all parts of his life. They witnessed the good parts, like miracles, and the truly horrible parts, like contemplating his own death in the Garden of Gethsemane. He also gave a high calling to a woman named Mary during a time when culture generally viewed women as property as much as people. Instead of living by this norm, Jesus honored her. As she cleaned his feet with her tears, dried them with her hair, and anointed him with perfume, everyone around Mary chastised her. They told her she was wasting good perfume, that she was foolish for throwing away an entire year's wages.

Jesus could have agreed with them. He could have cast Mary aside and associated himself with the men of higher status sitting around the table. He didn't do that, though. Instead, he gave her a new reputation. He said she'd not only done a beautiful thing for him, he said she'd be remembered wherever stories are told. He gave her a *legacy* in addition to a good name.

Think about that for a second. Can you imagine how Mary must have felt as she approached a renowned teacher, unprompted, in a setting where she was viewed as less-than? She must have been terrified, shaking as she wept on his feet. Now, can you envision how she would have felt while walking out of that room? Jesus gave her dignity! He disregarded an entire culture and changed her label from a wasteful woman to a living legend.

This is the reason the apostle Paul writes about having the same perspective as Christ. (Philippians 2) As he writes, "Do nothing from selfish ambition or conceit, but in humility count others more significant than yourselves," he's really suggesting that hollow actions won't cut it. He's encouraging us to see others as valuable, and in fact, to treat them as *more* significant than ourselves. In the same letter, Paul points out how we observe this seemingly upside-down principle in Christ's life:

> *[T]hough he was in the form of God, did not count equality with God a thing to be grasped, but emptied himself, by taking the form of a servant, being born in the likeness of men. And being found in human form, he humbled himself by becoming obedient to the point of death, even death on a cross. Therefore God has highly exalted him and bestowed on him the name that is above every name. (Philippians 2:6-9)*

This is critically important because none of us are static beings. We're always progressing into more humble, heavenly versions of ourselves, or more hollow, hellish caricatures of who God wants us to become. C.S. Lewis describes this saying:

> *…[A]ll your life long you are slowly turning… into a heavenly creature or a hellish creature: either into a creature that is in harmony with God, and with other creatures, and with itself, or else into one that is in a state of war and hatred with God, and with its fellow creatures, and with itself. To be the one kind of creature is heaven: that is, it is joy and peace and knowledge and power. To be the other means madness, horror, idiocy, rage, impotence, and eternal loneliness. Each of us at each moment is progressing to the one state of the other.*[22]

The question, then, is how are you encouraging the people around you? Can they see a better, future version of themselves when they're in your presence? Or do they feel like the short kid on the baseball team? It's worth considering because our answers ultimately reveal more about ourselves than others.

a rapping flight attendant

~ the simple things command the loudest praise ~
Ultimately, Mike created something entertaining from a totally ordinary experience. He didn't mind seeming strange at first, and for that, he brought us to our feet in praise and appreciation. Mike was doing his everyday job so excellently and creatively, we couldn't help but rise to recognize him.

———————

Have you ever seen the movie *Groundhog Day*, with Bill Murray? Murray plays a weatherman named Phil who's caught in some type of time loop. He relives the exact same day, every day. At first, Phil is cynical, frustrated, and even tries to escape the routine by driving off a cliff. By the end of the movie, he uses the repetition and his knowledge of the day's events for good. He infuses new energy into the weather report he's delivered dozens of times. He focuses on serving others, and finally, Phil finds love.

My life isn't too different from Phil's. Most of it is spent doing ordinary, everyday things like making toast and staying home on a Saturday when plans fall through. This isn't just my experience either. Scientifically speaking, our lives are far less interesting than we, or our social media feeds, like to admit.

Did you know fifty percent of English communication uses just 100 words?[23] Words like "the," "of," "this," and "that" make up most of our conversations. Even that one friend who always seems to be at parties, concerts, and taking vacations is more boring than you realize. A recent study found all people pick a group of twenty-five familiar locations – our house, our office, the gym, a particular restaurant – and we visit them over, and over, and over again.[24] To put a fine point on this, the Bureau of Labor Statistics found the average working professional spends twenty-one of twenty-four hours each day either sleeping, eating, working, or watching TV.[25]

So then, our lives are comprised by uninspiring routines, and I think we can all agree uninspiring tasks are the most difficult to invest our full effort and energy into. Consequently, it seems the people who live out the monotonous parts of their lives really, really well deserve the loudest praise. They're living the majority of their hours with a very high degree of excellence. They're squeezing the goodness of life right down to the pulp. That's something that deserves as much (if not more) glory than the news-worthy, singular moments of success we prefer to idolize.

I settled into aisle seat 10C – my preferred seat of choice on my last 100 flights. I popped in headphones as I waited for the rest of the passengers to board. A lady in bright pink lipstick sat to my right and smacked her gum, while a "bro" sat across the aisle to my left and recounted his epic weekend to another "bro" over the phone.

At this point in my travel career, I can recite the airlines' pre-flight safety speech word for word. I can even insert appropriately-timed pauses as the flight crew performs demonstrations for the seatbelt, oxygen mask, and life preserver. Knowing when that speech starts and stops tells me how much time I'll have with my laptop.

I turned down the volume in my headphones and tuned into the safety briefing. I started reciting the familiar words alongside the overhead speaker and at first, I heard what I expected to hear. But then, as I started listening with my ears instead of my memory, I noticed this speech sounded very unfamiliar.

Actually, it sounded horribly wrong. "Ladies and gentle... just right turn attention here! I mean, front of the cabin for a seatcard back pocket and 'monstration!"

I cringed. I stared at my feet to give our flight attendant some privacy. I felt bad for the guy. Clearly, he was new, and trying his best. He was probably pretty nervous to be giving the big speech during his first weeks on the job. It's awkward to screw up any type of public speaking, but butchering a pre-scripted, repetitious speech in front of 186 passengers is another level of embarrassment.

I stole a quick glance at the passengers around me. Everyone else had the same idea. They were inspecting their shoes, fixing their seatbelts, doing anything to avoid looking at the front of the plane. Then, we all heard something surprising – beatboxing.

The flight attendant bust into a lyrically-sound, audibly-pleasing rendition of the FAA-mandated script. He flew through the briefing with crisp and confident rhymes. He wove clever puns into the standard safety information. He topped off his lines with an ode to *Fresh Prince of Belair* by finishing with, "Mike's on the beat, so buckle yo seat. We 'bout to fly in the air, but don't get twisted 'cause this flight is rare."

The attendant, apparently named Mike, dropped his mic, threw his hands into the air, and leaned his head back. He let out a victorious, "Ahh," and our plane went nuts. Clapping, whistling, cheering, everyone gave it up for Mike. He'd just turned a mundane part of our week into something amusing. He converted a group of annoyed passengers into a captive audience. Even the bro to my left was using his phone to record the moment.

Mike gifted laughter to parents of small children dreading their flight. He offered relief to business travelers pushing through their Monday grind. He inspired his attendants to smile and serve with joy. Ultimately, Mike turned a totally ordinary experience into entertainment. He didn't mind seeming a little strange at first, and for that, he brought us to our feet in praise and appreciation. Mike did his everyday job so excellently and creatively we couldn't help but rise to recognize him.

Jesus spent nearly thirty years living out the everyday routines we're all familiar with. The Gospels pretty much skip from his birth to the start of his ministry, so I suppose his in-between years weren't too different from ours. If each of the four Gospel authors felt they could gloss over a few decades, in all likelihood, Jesus' weeks consisted of normal stuff like studying scripture, helping his father in the shop, and cracking jokes over a meal with friends.

That's an odd thought, isn't it? Jesus joking around and just being, well, human? Savior-of-the-world comes to earth, kills time, and laughs with family and friends. That's hard to wrap my mind around, but it's reality. God becoming fully human is among the most distinctive tenets of the Gospel message; no other god or divine figure has claimed to live like us (let alone bleed, hunger, or thirst like us).

That's why I think The Message's translation of John 1:14 gets it right when it says, "The Word became flesh and blood, and moved into the neighborhood." Jesus didn't just observe our lives from afar, looking down from shimmering clouds. His life wasn't just a highlight reel of miracles and shaping history on earth, either. He worked, walked, and waved hello to his neighbors, like we all do.

The apostle Paul knew that in both his dull moments and divine instances, Jesus' life was focused on doing his Father's will. He had this in mind when he wrote to the Corinthian church to say, "So whether you eat or drink or whatever you do, do it all for the glory of God." (1 Corinthians 10:31)

This would have been a strange thing for Paul's contemporaries, you see. Paul lived in an era of religious role models who only wanted to appear righteous. They paraded their charitable giving in the streets. They stood front and center in the synagogue to pray. They invested their best if others watched. They seemed holy, but really, they had no concern for the condition of their hearts. Only their reputations.

Jesus, by contrast, was only concerned with God's reputation – his glory. It's how he lived every moment of every week, and Paul holds this as the standard in his letter. God's glory is the goal of living, without any room for negotiation. Paul chooses the most basic tasks of life (eating and drinking) to leave us no say in the matter. Simply put, there's *never* a time to *not* live for God's glory.

This is a difficult thing to do, and that's probably understating it. Jesus-like excellence is exhausting. It goes against everything I desire. I'd rather serve as CEO of a Fortune 500 company than clean airline seats and repeat the same safety speech over and over again. However, according to Paul, these roles hold equal dignity if we use every moment on the job to make much of God's name. In this sense, Paul says excellence isn't measured by status or success. It's not about being *the* best, only *my* best, to increase God's glory.

Ultimately, simple things done with excellence will cause God to one day say, "Well done, good and faithful servant. You have been faithful over a little; I will set you over much." (Matthew 25:23) So we may see groundhog-day routines as tedious, tiresome, and a good reason to look for shortcuts, but humble moments give us an opportunity to do our job well. And when we do, we might not hear a plane full of people clapping, but our Heavenly Father who sits on a throne far higher than any airplane will be cheering us on.

lock the doors

~ little inconveniences create big frustrations ~
Life's pressures may produce character, but the little frustrations test how solid that character truly is. When we're pricked – not pressed – we discover just how mature we've become.

The nonprofit WATERisLIFE created a splash after one of its marketing campaigns featured kids in third-world countries reading first-world tweets. Each tweet shared a first-world "problem," contrasted by the setting in which it was read. For example, one kid read, "I hate when my leather seats aren't heated," while sitting on a pile of rubble. In another clip, a twenty-something said, "I hate when my house is so big I need two wireless routers," while standing next to a shack barely taller than himself.

The campaign went viral because it communicated a serious message in a wholly relatable way. While I've never wondered about my basic, everyday needs, whether I'll eat or have electricity, I know what it's like to feel frustrated by little hiccups in my week. Hiccups like running out of milk before filling my cereal bowl, or my beard trimmer running out of battery while shaving.

Nobody loves lopsided facial hair, so the point isn't we should feel bad if our basic needs are met, or that third-world countries can't relate to first-world problems. Rather, when access to clean water is our reference point, a skewed grain-to-dairy ratio in our cereal bowl should be no big deal. We shouldn't cry over spilled milk, as the saying goes.

And yet, I do. Regularly. Minor hassles tend to aggravate me most. Trivial things like someone using a dozen coupons at the grocery store checkout annoy me far too much. While the impact of these moments on my life is rather low, they send my blood pressure sky high. Selfishly, I fixate on my disrupted schedule, and I ignore the possibility that a few dollars may be worth a half-hour's pay to that coupon-clipper.

It's a strange thing. While genuine hardship brings out the best in me, life's little speedbumps reveal the worst of me. I come alive with grit and delight when life's ugly trials sink their teeth into me. I'm collected under pressure, but I crumble like a schoolchild with a bee sting when the little things don't go my way. It's one of those odd realities that keeps showing up in my life: mild inconveniences frustrate me most.

―――

You have a junk drawer in your house, right? A drawer that accumulates all kinds of rubber bands, charging cables, scraps of paper? Most people do, but I can't tolerate mess, so instead, I created a junk drawer for my weeks – Sundays.

It's a bad habit. I've tried to kick it, but I typically save a whole list of tasks for the very day I should reserve for church and family. Inevitably, I wake up on Sundays trying to write books, ride bikes, knock out house projects, and get a head-start on work, all while spending "quality" time with my wife. Basically, I cram a week of to-do's into the last day of the week and expect it all to fit.

It's not that I'm a procrastinator. Rather, I'm only as content as the projects I accomplish, and I overestimate my ability to complete them in a reasonable amount of time. As those two factors coalesce, I frantically shuffle around the house trying to make the impossible work out, venting my inevitable frustration when I can't.

I thought I could change this a few Sundays ago. I was in the middle of training for an Ironman, which is a triathlon that demands a great deal of focus on performance and long workouts, but I asked Erin if she'd like to ride bikes together. Our last ride had ended in tears, and I wanted to make it up to her. Long story short, I wanted to ride fast on heavily-trafficked roads, while Erin preferred a leisurely pace on the bike trails, and compromise wasn't how I handled that situation.

"We can take our time, riding through the rich neighborhoods," I enticed her. It's one of our hobbies; we cruise by mansions lining nearby golf courses, musing about which features we'll build into our one-day dream home. I wanted to show her that despite my training schedule, this ride would be different.

"You know we don't ride at the same pace, right?" Erin tested me. "And I don't like busy roads?"

"Yes, yes," I confirmed.

"And you're fine sticking with me on side streets?"

"Yep."

"Even though you're training?" She pressed.

"Yes! C'mon. It'll be fun," I said.

Riding with Erin brings back sweet memories of our early days. In addition to running by and swimming in Lake Michigan, riding bikes was one of our first dates. I guess you could say spandex brought us together. I have to admit, however, nostalgia wasn't my only motive that morning. I was feeling tempted to multi-task. I figured riding together meant checking "quality time" off my to-do list, alongside my daily training. What's better than the smell of efficiency in the morning?

"You really think we can ride and get to church on time?" Erin said once more with a note of skepticism.

"Yeah, no problem."

"And you know we have to get there early, right? We're signed up to serve today," she reminded me.

"We'll be fine if we leave now." Truthfully, she had me on that one. I hadn't forgotten, but I didn't factor it into my plan. Arriving on time wasn't on my list of priorities.

"Alright," Erin smiled. "You get the bikes ready, I'll go change."

Ten minutes later, we were ready to roll. We don't have a keypad for our garage door, so after Erin wheeled her bike outside, I pressed the button and ran toward her. I ducked below the door as it closed behind me and yelled, "Ready!"

"You grabbed a house key, right?" Erin inquired.

"I thought you were going to?" That's the line I use when something crossed my mind, but I assumed Erin, who's far more planful than I, probably had it covered.

"I didn't, but that's fine. We can use our spare," she suggested, referring to a small key hidden in our backyard.

I knew I should have put that key back.

I kicked myself, realizing that was the exact thought I'd had yesterday, after letting myself into the house with our spare key.

"We can't, actually. I used it yesterday. You were out shopping when I got back from my ride," I shrugged.

"So, we're locked out?"

"Maybe, but let's just ride," I directed. First things were first in my mind. We could deal with unlocking our doors afterward. While it'd definitely mean arriving late to church, it wasn't my priority.

"Nate, no. If we can't get inside, we need to call someone."

I drew a deep breath. "Well, let me just check the back door and windows. Maybe we left one unlocked."

I knew very well I'd locked them, but I wasn't willing to negotiate my plan for the day. I reappeared in the driveway two minutes later, attempting to convince Erin we should stay on schedule, despite officially being locked out. "I can call someone while we ride," I offered.

"How?" She wasn't convinced.

"We'll ride slow. I'll google a locksmith on my phone as we go."

I grew restless. I could sense my finely-arranged morning slipping through my fingers. Like a train conductor wanting to hit each station at just the right time, I knew each minute spent standing on the driveway meant one less riding. That, in turn, would domino my agenda, offsetting the time I'd allotted for my other projects.

"What if you need to sign something? Locksmiths can't just open up a house without the owner there," Erin reasoned. "Call someone first, and we'll see when they can get here."

The third locksmith I tried answered his phone, and said he'd be at our house in twenty minutes. *This really sucks, but twenty minutes isn't terrible,* I thought. I hung up and started re-assigning projects to different time slots in my mind. If I could squeeze my timetable by a few minutes here and there, I'd still achieve maximum efficiency.

Have you ever seen someone catch the speed wobbles? Whether it's a skateboard, bike, or motorcycle, once a small pebble or obstacle starts the wobbles, they grow in intensity and oscillate the rider farther and farther to each side until eventually, the rider crashes. I wasn't on my bike, but I got the wobbles nonetheless. One small setback – locked doors – threw me off course and I never recovered.

After the agreed-upon twenty minutes came and went and there was no locksmith in sight, the wobbles worsened. "Where's this guy at?" I asked incredulously, sitting in my spandex and tapping my bike cleats on our front porch.

"Did he stop for a four-course breakfast or something?"

Erin didn't indulge me. She let me sulk because sometimes, trying to blow out a fire only stokes the flames.

"Do you tip locksmiths?" I continued my rant. "I hope you do, just so I can decide to *not* give him a tip for showing up late."

Eventually, Erin tried to console me. "Look at it this way. Now we get to just hang out and enjoy each other's company."

It was nice a thing to say, but rather than enjoy what I had left – time with my wife – I could only whine about what had been taken from me. Worse, as I considered how frustrated I felt, the fact I felt frustrated really frustrated me. It was a nasty spiral.

I continued tapping my foot as I tried to pull out of my tailspin. While I generally relish the experiences that most find insufferable – slogging through the Amazon jungle, gritting out 100-mile bike rides – one little speedbump had completely knocked me off center. I've endured some pretty unforgiving conditions, but a 45-minute delay? Forget about it. I was as upset as a toddler being told ice cream isn't an actual meal.

I wish I could say that changed. That I adjusted my attitude and spent the rest of the day in quality time with Erin. But after the locksmith came and went, I stewed over how my master plan had been foiled. It wasn't until I crawled into bed that night that I felt sorry. I'd subjected Erin to my sour mood, so I apologized to her. When I did, she was quick to articulate what I was slow to realize.

With equal parts laugh and groan she said, "You're really good at staying calm when life is intense, but you're really bad when little stuff throws you off." Then, she shared what I really needed to hear. "Just remember when we have kids, you can't get frustrated when days don't go your way anymore."

Ouch. The hardest part about hearing those words was Erin was absolutely right. I can withstand life's serious setbacks, but I sweat the small stuff. Which is an issue, because life's pressures may produce character, but little frustrations test just how solid that character truly is. When we're pricked – not pressed – we discover how mature we've grown.

Forgetting our house keys opened my eyes to see I wasn't as mature as I thought. At my core, I prioritized myself. My time, my goals, my ambition. These things came first in my mind, so when they were second in reality, I whined about it. That needed to change because newborns don't operate by their parents' plans, and as it turned out, Erin was already ready for that. She'd had a few years of practice caring for a husband who could act like one hairy, oversized toddler.

In the opening words of James' letter, he writes, "Count it all joy, my brothers, when you meet trials of various kinds, for you know that the testing of your faith produces steadfastness." (James 1:2-3) Steadfastness is significant to James because he says with enough time, it's the virtue which creates "perfect and complete" followers of Christ. In other words, and to use a gran cliché, he says time and pressure form perfect diamonds.

Although steep, it makes sense perfection is James' standard. Most scholars agree he was Jesus' brother, and his writing mirrors the famed Sermon on The Mount in which Jesus says, "You therefore must be perfect, as your heavenly Father is perfect." (Matthew 5:48)

"Therefore" is preceded in the sermon by a long list of imperatives concerning anger, lust, divorce, integrity, revenge, love, and a description of the characteristics God blesses. James describes that blessing a few sentences later. He writes, "Blessed is the man who remains steadfast under trial, for when he has stood the test he will receive the crown of life, which God has promised to those who love him." (James 1:12)

Ultimately, James is pointing out there's a specific end goal behind us remaining steadfast and growing in character. This idea of enduring for a purpose is repeated time and time again by the Bible's authors. Paul, for example, asks the Corinthians, "Do you not know that in a race all the runners run, but only one receives the prize? So run that you may obtain it." (1 Corinthians 9:24)

This is serious business. Our calling as followers of Christ is one of great weight. The standard to which Jesus, James, Paul, and God himself hold us is perfection, attaining a crown, and the first-place prize. It's a solemn charge which, without doubt, will require us to struggle.

Fortunately, we all have the capacity to sustain a great deal of pain. It just comes down to the purpose behind the pain. But in today's digital and consumer age, pain stands in stark contrast to a far more familiar experience – inconvenience. It's why first-world problems are funny; they're common and relatable. Yet, far too frequently, the root of inconvenience is not enduring for an eternal prize or crown of life. It's selfishness. Different from "trials of many kinds," which accompany greater purpose, life's little hassles don't always have much meaning. Sometimes, our plans are blown off course by nothing more than locked doors, and selfishly, how could there be any purpose in things not going our way?

This means trivial encounters are often an accurate measuring stick for how we've progressed in our calling to Christ-like perfection. When we live for ourselves, our threshold for feeling frustrated is dramatically reduced. Or in the words of Henry Ward Beecher, "No man is more cheated than the selfish man." An oversized ego magnifies small setbacks into personal attacks, which quickly turns mild inconveniences into the most severe frustrations.

Looking back, a set of locked doors opened my eyes to see just how selfishly I view my time, and how that needed to change before our first child. While I still wobble more than I'd like, I'm working on seeing life's little speedbumps as a chance to slow down and double-check what I'm living for – God's call to perfection, or my own purposes.

overalls on an airplane

~ the more we consume, the less satisfied we feel ~
Jesus pointed out that a poverty of possessions removed the possibility we'd look to stuff to satisfy us. Without glimmering treasure blinding us from God's invitation, we'll find a full life in his kingdom.

At the start of the twentieth century, corporate executives discovered a new approach to kickstarting our economy – consumption. Wartime production pulled our economy out of steep stagnation and depressions in the '20s and '40s, but after military demand for supplies declined, entire industries needed new buyers. Buyers create demand, which sustains production, increases employment, grows wages, and increases spending power. It's a prosperous cycle.

A new type of working professional was created to influence millions to spend billions. "Admen," the nickname for those in the male-dominated advertising industry, were paid to ensure shoppers shelled out top dollar for the latest and greatest consumer products. At the outset, admen appealed to our sense of nobility. Living as a middle-class consumer became a patriotic duty. Buying American-made products was akin to doing your part to uphold the American way of life.

In this way, Admen conditioned people to associate unending spending with good morals, not bad banking. Simon Patten, who was an economist at the Wharton School of Business in the early 1900s, put it like this:

> *I tell my students to spend all they have and borrow more and spend that... It is no evidence of loose morality when a stenographer, earning eight or ten dollars a week, appears dressed in clothing that takes nearly all of her earnings to buy. It is a sign of her growing moral development.*[26]

Simon said if you're truly an ambitious and upright person, that should be revealed by your possessions. Your character is shown in your clothes, so convince employers of your honesty and good nature with how you dress.

Eventually, admen realized they could kick our spending into overdrive if they shifted from virtues and morals to a "needs" economy. Instead of "wants," products were positioned as must-have fundamentals for human life. They accomplished this by creating emotional bonds with buyers at a time when federal programs eased access to credit, gave families the chance to own a home, and created a whole new market of consumers.

For example, fertilizer was no longer something to turn brown patches of grass into a uniformly green lawn. It was rebranded as the ticket to neighborly acceptance. A brown lawn tells neighbors you're an incompetent, lazy slob. A green lawn signals you're a capable, pleasing fellow. Social acceptance is an internal *need,* while a green lawn is an external *want.*

So why the history lesson? Well, things haven't gotten any better.

Technologies like ride-sharing platforms were supposed to shrink production, reduce our negative impact on the environment, and enable us to live with less. Instead, the opposite has happened. We work longer hours, create more carbon emissions, and carry larger consumer debts than ever before. This may not seem like a big deal at first. It probably feels normal, but that's what's concerning. Christians no longer stick out because we manage our consumption differently – forgoing a new phone so we can give more to our local church, for example. We blend in when we're supposed to be swimming upstream.

The airport loudspeaker cut through the music playing in my headphones. "Sorry folks, we need y'all to sit back down. We found some mechanical issues with the aircraft and we're not sure when our new departure time will be, but we'll keep you updated."

I knew the drill. I boarded sixty-three flights in the six-month stretch prior to this trip, so I'd heard those ominous words a few times before. I hadn't heard it in the Dallas airport however, so I guess it was a first of sorts.

While I stood in line, someone had pounced on my gate-side seat. It was one of the good ones with an outlet and a window, too. I collected my duffel and shuffled past the throng of roller-bags near the gate, looking for a new place to make camp. Hopefully I'd only be there a few more minutes, but who knew? "Mechanical" isn't the word you want to hear when talking about delayed flights.

I found a pair of vacant seats a few rows away. I settled into a black pleather chair and felt an unpleasant warmth spread across my back. A nervous flier had most likely sat there. I leaned forward from the seatback and grabbed my phone to text a friend, Jeff.

"Dude," I tapped out a quick message. "I might be landing in

Denver later than planned..."

Jeff and his fiancé were flying in to go skiing with Erin and me over the weekend. My flight was supposed to land two hours before theirs, but after the gate agent announced, "We're looking into other aircraft to get everyone to their final destinations safely," I was just hoping to get home that day.

"Hey, can I join you?"

I looked up from my phone to see who was speaking. I wasn't expecting to see what I saw – a man in his late thirties wearing a sheepish grin and an equally goofy pair of snow pants. He pointed to my duffel bag, which occupied the chair next to me, implying he wanted me to move it for him.

His bib-style snow pants rose over his shoulders and clipped in the front. They had extra padding that bunched around his knees and waist, like the kind parents buy for toddlers learning to ski. I was confused as to why someone would wear snow pants in an airport, a Texas airport of all places, before remembering I was headed home to Denver.

"Oh, yeah, sure," I mumbled. "You're going skiing this weekend, huh?" I asked as I moved my bag from the chair. Maybe it was his insulated overalls that had been incubating my seat.

"Yes! It's my first time, believe it or not," he said emphatically.

That wasn't hard to believe at all, but I let him continue. "I'm meeting some friends. I don't think they'll be very happy to see me if we arrive too late, though," he sighed.

"Yeah, I have some friends waiting on me, too," I shared. "But your first time, that's exciting. Which mountain are you skiing?"

"Not sure. They say they're going to watch the weather and we'll go where the snow's good. Maybe Gunnison, or something like that. Heard of it?" He asked.

"Sure, I was there a few weeks ago. That's some ambitious skiing for your first time."

"Wherever's fine with me. I just can't wait to get there," he beamed as he kicked his cowboy boots out in front of him and continued speaking.

"I don't know what you do, but I work in the oil fields. Skiing's rare there. Never thought I'd go until some buddies moved and told me to visit. Never seen snow either, so I figured I might as well get used to this gear."

He thumbed his overall straps, snapping them against his chest. I laughed. It sounded like his friends had some intense skiing in store for him, and I could only appreciate his eager naivety. He was wearing his overalls on an airplane, after all.

"You'll have fun," I assured him. "It'll be different than Texas, but you'll have a blast."

I looked around the gate area after my new friend grew quiet. A TV mounted in the corner caught my eye. A liquor commercial featuring impressive people doing impressive things rolled along before the words, "Never Stop, Never Settle," hung on the screen. My first thought was to question the apparent link between liquor and extraordinary accomplishments. My next thought was born from the dichotomy of the tagline, "Never Stop, Never Settle," and my new friend.

On one hand, I'd just met a man so chock-full of delight for bunny hills and beat-up rental skis he'd decided to wear his snow pants in the airport. On the other was an ad placing the ideals of incessant achievement and relentless consumption on full display. The commercial said "more" is the answer. Regardless of whether I felt fulfilled or hollow, the nature of the word "never" suggested that settling is to be avoided at all costs. Contentment shouldn't be an option (and of course, if living by their mantra ever left me empty, I could just pick up a bottle of alcohol).

Yet, the goofy grin and overalls next to me begged to differ. As I was sulking about a flight delay, Mr. Overalls was smiling. He was the happier man between us, and the major difference between him and I was he'd never been skiing, while I started at four years old. As a result, the inconvenience of our flight delay put a damper on my weekend while Mr. Overalls excitedly awaited the snow.

To be honest, I felt a little jealous of him. I wanted that first-time feeling glowing inside me too. Most of my weeks are spent in a never-settle mentality. I waste too much time thinking about "if-then" scenarios. "If I could just..." or "If I could only..." followed by some "then" and a false promise. "If I could just earn six-figures, *then* I'd spend more time with family." "If I could just drop five pounds, *then* I'd feel more confident in my body." "If I could only buy a slightly nicer car/tv/couch/watch, *then* I'll start saving."

If restlessness is a crime, I'm among the guiltiest offenders. Like, life-sentence guilty. Anyone who knows me knows Nate without another goal or project is Nate at his worst. I spend my time trying to fill an insatiable void with more things and more-extraordinary experiences. "If I could just..."

I don't think this challenge is limited to over-achievers, though. I think we all need a Mr. Overalls approach. Consuming more, whether it's more experiences, products, or even new relationships, is a bottomless pit that never contents us. "More" never creates the thrill of heading to the bunny slopes after working in the oil fields. But if we trust consumption never equates satisfaction, we can start to find what will truly fill us.

———

Jesus spoke a lot about filling the holes in our hearts. He said we try to plug these holes with all kinds of stuff when what we really need is a savior. In fact, he said we'd truly know where our heart's affections lie by how much we consume while instructing, "Do not store up for yourselves treasures on earth... But store up for yourselves treasures in heaven... For where your treasure is, there your heart will be also." (Matthew 6:19-21) Admen may say better clothes mean better morals, but the one who truly knows us said our possessions reveal our priorities: God's, or ours.

Jesus totally turned our world's link between consumption and contentment on its head. He went so far as to say, "Blessed are you who are poor, for yours is the kingdom of God." (Luke 6:20) Notice he didn't say blessed are you who have "enough," or blessed are you who "settle" (let alone you who never settle). He pointed out that a poverty of possessions removes the possibility we'll look to stuff to satisfy us. Without glimmering treasure blinding us from God's invitation, we'll be able find a full life in his kingdom.

Jesus knew this is easier said than done, by the way. On another occasion, he exposed just how strong the draw of treasure and wealth and possessions actually is. So strong, in fact, that Jesus said it's nearly impossible for a rich man to find God's kingdom. As a wealthy man approached Jesus, he asked, "Teacher, what good deed must I do to have eternal life?" After Jesus told him to keep God's commandments, and he said he had, Jesus replied, "If you would be perfect, go, sell what you possess and give to the poor, and you will have treasure in heaven; and come, follow me." Then, here's what happened next:

> *When the young man heard this he went away sorrowful, for he had great possessions. And Jesus said to his disciples, "Truly,*

> *I say to you, only with difficulty will a rich person enter the kingdom of heaven. Again I tell you, it is easier for a camel to go through the eye of a needle than for a rich person to enter the kingdom of God. (Matthew 19:16-24)*

Believe it or not, the man's riches weren't the central issue here. Instead, Jesus revealed that the man's "great possessions" had crowded his heart. He hadn't left any room for God. His good deeds were just an attempt to have it all. He wanted to find eternal life later, and hang onto his treasure now. Deep down, the rich man knew that approach was falling short. Otherwise, he wouldn't have asked Jesus his question in the first place.

Jesus' response tells us finding eternal life, which satisfies our hearts' ultimate longings, only happens when we've made room for God. Not only that, we must place God first because finding his kingdom is not as simple as following his commands. It's a matter of our priorities. Had the rich man been willing to sell his possessions, he would have found the kingdom – he would have finally valued his savior over his stuff.

Generation after generation of Bible authors reinforced that as long as we have God, we have it all. The writer of Hebrews encouraged us, "…be content with what you have, because God has said, 'Never will I leave you; never will I forsake you.'" (Hebrews 13:5) Even Solomon, the one guy in history who literally had it all, and I mean everything from riches to land to sex to power and wisdom, said, "He who loves money will not be satisfied with money, nor he who loves wealth with his income." (Ecclesiastes 5:10) Solomon knew "if-then" statements never work out. "If I could just get a little more, then I'd be happy…" is deceiving.

In the end, stuff never lasts, and more never satisfies. Even the thrill of throwing on overalls and cruising down the mountain for the first time fades away. So, the question we're left with is this. Will we buy culture's narrative of consumption, or will we make room for Jesus to finally and wholly fill us?

a stranger you

Have you ever seen that video where you're told to count how many passes a group of people tossing a basketball complete before time expires? If so, you know that at the end, the narrator plays back the footage and reveals there was a gorilla dancing in the background the whole time. It was in plain sight yet completely hidden. I was indignant the first time I watched it. I was genuinely frustrated because I'd like to think I'm an observant person. That I can pick up on messages as overt as a dancing gorilla.

In reality, I think this video is a good illustration of how our relationship with God plays out. He shows up in conspicuous ways over and over again, but he works in ways we don't expect, so we miss him. We pray for patience; he sends us locked doors. We want to love others; we get frozen pipes. We ask to grow in kindness, and we get the chocolate lab we never wanted (but now adore!). In response we wonder, *Where are you God? Why haven't you shown up?* Meanwhile, God's thinking, *I'm standing here in a gorilla suit. What more do you want?*

It's easy to question the answers God gives us even though he explicitly says his ways are not our ways and his plans are not our plans. When a lesson feels backward or uncomfortable to us, it's natural to reject it. I mean, who enjoys disruptions, paying invoices, and reworking our lives around others? Surely nobody. And we certainly can prioritize ourselves and collect on what we're owed. But when we await God's seemingly-strange ways of working in our world, and we take him at his word when he says he has "plans to prosper you and not to harm you, plans to give you hope and a future," then and only then will we find what we never expected. (Jeremiah 29:11) Peace for our anxiety, contentment for our restlessness, and joy during our darkest days – everything our world craves but will never find apart from God.

Lest it sound like God promises a panacea for our problems, choosing to align our lives with his design means sticking out. It means looking strange to a culture that sees faith as something outdated, biased, bigoted, and banned from school classrooms. Can you imagine telling a neighbor who asked how you're doing, "It's been a tough week, but I have hope because this is when God's power is made perfect." (2 Corinthians 12:9) The thought of being labeled the odd, religious nut is a scary thing.

Jesus took this a step further when he said:

> *If the world hates you, keep in mind that it hated me first. If you belonged to the world, it would love you as its own. As it is, you do not belong to the world, but I have chosen you out of the world. That is why the world hates you... They will treat you this way because of my name, for they do not know the one who sent me. (John 15:18-19, 21)*

Hate is a few degrees more intense than strange. There have been times when I've avoided sharing "the reason for the hope [I] have" for fear I'll be hated. (1 Peter 3:15) I've withheld for dread of being misunderstood. I think the reason is one we can all relate to. Religious or not, we all yearn to find our place in this world. We long to belong at a deep, soul level.

But while we've been trying to fit in, truth is, God's been asking us to stand out. He wants us to be a people set apart, a city on a hill who looks and acts differently because ultimately, our place isn't in this world. We were made for another. One in which Jesus promises, "I will see you again and you will rejoice, and no one will take away your joy." (John 16:22) And this is perhaps the most backward lesson of all. When we stand out in this world, we find our place in God's kingdom.

In what ways may God be asking you to stand out for his glory? Take a moment to talk with him. What distractions might prevent you from seeing and hearing what he has for you? Pause and consider this. When you get his message, what fears or anxieties might hold you back from following him? Will you give into them, or will this be the start of a stranger you?

If you enjoyed *That Seems Strange,* make sure to subscribe at natenasralla.com for updates on the latest books, blogs, and giveaways. You can also read an excerpt from Nate's book *Living Forward, Looking Backward* on the next page.

NATE NASRALLA
LIVING FORWARD LOOKING BACKWARD

*uncover more meaning in your
ordinary, everyday life*

introduction

Are you living a meaningful life? If we're honest, most of us will answer "not sure," or "not really." It's not an easy question to emphatically answer, "yes!" The reality is that our days are often filled with more routines than grand adventures, and we're not fulfilled by the common things in life. Eating cereal, sitting in traffic, and staying home on a Saturday when plans fall through won't make the headlines and highlights displayed on our social media feeds. Instead, we're captivated by the extraordinary things which will never happen within a normal week – getting a big promotion, finishing a marathon, buying a new car.

I believe, however, that your regular life is far more significant than you realize. There is deep meaning hiding in your everyday conversations and ordinary interactions – you just can't see it in the moment. You and I both need a framework to help us uncover more of the meaning in our ordinary, everyday lives. We need more stories.

We love stories, you see. It's how we're wired. Well-crafted stories stick with us. They allow us to recall life lessons in a memorable way. They also help us see the big picture during frustrating and disappointing circumstances. We even build our identities around stories. Where we came from, where we're going, the highs and lows – it's all part of the narratives we tell to the world.

When you begin to look at your life as one big story and recount your past, you'll discover that meaning often looks different from what we would have expected. Life's universal truths repeatedly show up in ways that feel strange to us. For example, it's easiest to hurt those we love most. The smallest steps achieve the biggest goals. Disappointing beginnings create happy endings. That all feels a little backward, right?

I noticed this after cycling through a rapid series of major life changes within a single year. After moving cities, merging companies, and getting married, all around the same time, I needed to process the change in a healthy way. Writing is therapeutic to me, so I began to create short stories from a series of notes I had jotted down during the preceding years. Whenever something special or notable stuck out to me, I opened the Notes app on my phone and I wrote down a quote I read, something a friend said over dinner, or a thought I had while jogging.

As I wrote and then connected these stories in a timeline, I noticed one consistent theme in every season of my life – paradox. A paradox is a feeling or experience that appears strange or backward in the moment, but it actually makes complete sense in the larger context.

I've come to believe our lives are shaped by these two principles: paradox and storytelling. You'll see it's true when you look back on your own life's events in one, overarching story. You'll discover there is a greater, unseen purpose behind it all, even when your circumstances don't feel significant. When life doesn't make sense, it's because the plotline is still unfolding in ways you don't expect. I wrote this book to help you see how these two principles are at work in your life.

Now, the great thing about stories is they're universal – you have a life story, as does everyone else. And because every story ever written contains conflict, we know that we'll all encounter conflict at some point in our lives. Sooner or later, we find ourselves facing a crossroads, difficult decisions, or relational strain. In these moments of tension, we don't often understand the long-term significance of what's developing. We rarely value the experience as we live it. It's only after making it to the other side of conflict that we can look back, find meaning, and apply a new lesson to our lives as we keep on living forward.

While I've watched friends navigate conflicts that happen to them – illness, death, unexpected tragedies – my greatest struggles seem to rise up from within me – anxiety, fear, loneliness. Conflict in my story has felt like friendly-fire. Something that's unexpected, bewildering, and it leaves you uncertain about how to fight back.

As you continue to read, you'll see that my story's conflicts continually leave me saying, "This again?" I face the battles I thought I had already fought (and won) time and time again. It's demoralizing to feel like I'm always re-fighting the same battles. Nonetheless, I've never kept a daily journal nor committed much time to reflect on my life, so I often repeat the errors from which I should have already learned. As you read on, my hope is that you learn from these mistakes.

More importantly, my hope is that you discover how these two concepts, the framework of storytelling and the principle of paradox, will help you uncover more meaning in the ordinary, everyday moments of your own life.

If you come from a faith-based worldview, you'll notice that these two elements consistently and coherently align with the Christian worldview. If you don't come from any faith-based worldview, keep reading. Understanding these elements will help you discover greater meaning in your everyday life too, regardless of your religious beliefs.

costa rican watermelons

- slow down and you'll see more in life -

I didn't know that we'd end up there. It just sort of happened. So ultimately, after deciding to slow down, I was actually seeing more of the country and absorbing more of our trip.

The majority of my days feel like plain vanilla ice cream. Unremarkable and predictable. I eat, get dressed, commute, and spend time transitioning from one routine to another. Can you relate? It would seem, then, that breaking from my daily schedule to backpack Latin America for weeks with a good friend would have produced all kinds of new learning and maturity. In reality, the excess of new experiences and photogenic moments distracted me from an important reality. I missed the fact that we don't need exotic trips to learn from life. We just need to look around. I found that when I finally stopped hurrying from one adventure to the next, I began to grow. I actually saw more of the country by slowing down.

"Dude. This. Sucks," Greg said as he lay out on the hard tile floor at the Ft. Lauderdale airport. He rolled over as I nodded in agreement. I glanced at my watch. It was about 1:00 a.m. We had been lying on the ground for three hours thanks to a flight delay, and we weren't interested in experimenting with the only restaurant in the terminal. It served warm beer and "Chicago" style hot dogs from rotating warming trays.

"Yeah... not quite the start we were hoping for," I laughed half-heartedly.

I was too tired to laugh, but I had to feign some excitement like it was all just a part of the adventure. Greg and I had $4,000 in traveling money between us, and we'd decided to travel to Nicaragua and Costa Rica for one month before we each started new jobs. I had been hired to work for a consulting firm in Chicago. Greg was headed off to work for a big energy company in Philadelphia. It seemed appropriate that a new adventure would precede new cities, new jobs, and new paychecks.

Here's a travel tip for you. If you're planning to travel with only $2,000 to your name, you need to start with a fair amount of confidence that you won't run out of money along the way. So, to save for food and hostels, Greg and I decided we'd book our flights to Managua, Nicaragua on some budget airline known for canceling or changing flights without warning.

Clearly, our idea wasn't as smart as it first sounded.

I reached into my backpack and grabbed a small folder of papers. "We planned this trip to a T, but I guess that doesn't mean we'll get to follow the plan," I said to Greg. I realized then that backpacking requires an odd blend of meticulousness when planning a route, but spontaneity to actually travel it.

"Now boarding: All passengers to Managua. Please, line up near the gate."

"Thank heavens. Let's go, Greg."

Once aboard our plane, I settled into my seat and slipped my sandals off my feet. I stretched out to the whopping twenty inches of legroom that tin-can-of-an-airplane allowed, and I closed my eyes. I wondered if we'd encounter more setbacks once we landed in Nicaragua, or if we'd have a smoother trip from that point forward. The engines spooled up and the pilot taxied out to the runway through the humid summer air. I created future Instagram captions in my head while drifting off to sleep, "Here we are diving into an active volcano to catch alligators..."

"So, man, what do you wanna do?"

Greg set his phone on his chest and lifted his head from his pillow, awaiting my response. We had done a lot of traveling already, and we had generally stuck to our plan. We checked off cities and experiences from our list, one after the other. We actually did climb an active volcano (sadly, there were no alligators), surfed next to small sharks, and watched the sun set over the ocean while eating tacos from a little lady grilling on a roadside cart. By all standards, we had moved from one extraordinary adventure to another. Even traveling from city to city was interesting. We'd throw our backpacks atop a 10-passenger van and cruise the narrow streets, taking it all in.

Despite it all, I had grown restless.

Sitting on our hostel beds, I found myself looking for the next big thing. I didn't feel full. I just wanted to do, see, and explore more. I felt like our trip, if not built on one bold moment after another, wouldn't be that epic pre-wife-and-kids trip you recall with a longing fondness as you try to calm a baby that's crying and pooping at 3 a.m.

"I'm not sure man, but I know I want to do something. Why don't we just go outside? We can walk around until we find something. Or at least until something finds us."

I framed it as a suggestion, but before Greg could reply, I had already put on my sandals and sat at the edge of my bed. I was halfway to the door by the time Greg shrugged his shoulders as if to say, "Sure man, whatever you want."

He would have given me the same shrug regardless. That's Greg. He was the ultimate travel companion. Up for whatever and content with anything from playing games on his cell phone to jumping off the tallest bungee platform in Latin America (which we also did). If I was honest with myself, I'd have admitted I envied Greg's ability to enjoy our ordinary moments just as much as the high-octane ones. It was clear Greg's ease would sustain him after our trip, continuing in his everyday life at work and home.

I wanted that inner calm.

Throughout our trip, Greg's needs were pretty modest. He focused on two things; finding one good bottle of wine and ensuring we had enough capital left in our bank accounts to buy it. That's all he cared about. My mind, on the other hand, was an unquenchable firestorm. As soon as we finished one activity, I was already burning for the next and figuring out the fastest way to get there. Instead of relishing the high of a new experience, I was over that event, past its memory, and yearning for something different.

Greg slapped on some sandals and pulled on a yellow tank top he'd bought for a dollar on the beach. Then, we left the hostel to cure my restlessness. We wandered down the county road for fifteen minutes before Greg finally asked, "Where are we going?"

We had drifted by the fire station, the local park, a grocery store, and we'd pretty much covered everything our little Costa Rican mountain town offered. "To that corner store," I pointed straight ahead. "I'm thirsty. You want something? Maybe they have ice cream."

We hadn't found anything to do, but I figured I'd drive Greg nuts if we just kept wandering around until we stumbled across something unique enough to satiate my hunger for adventure. I stepped into the little store and scanned the rows of snacks. I saw a little woman sitting behind the counter, quietly counting coins and ignoring us as we stepped inside.

"Hola," I said as I walked toward a standing refrigerator. I eased the glass door open and tossed Greg a frosty bottle of Coca-Cola.

"We're looking for something to do. Is there anything you recommend?" I asked her in Spanish.

Have you ever seen the movie Pirates of the Caribbean? Where the pirates become part of the ship's mast and railings after living at sea for so long? It was the same deal with this woman. I guessed she had been sitting on that same stool since she was a teenager, restocking rows of chips for decades. I assumed that after her years of shop-tending and coin-counting, she'd know more about the town than Google and a guidebook combined.

I leveraged my Spanish to learn that not far up the road, while the tourists paid ninety dollars to relax in fancy hot springs fed by the Arenal volcano, the locals had their own hangout in the same thermal streams. The shop tender said that if we journeyed up the hillside for a half-mile to a wooded entrance hidden on the side of the county road and passed a few low-hanging trees, there would be a clearing that opened into a set of naturally formed rock baths (simple directions, right?). Each cascaded into the next, all fed by the volcano's heat, creating a hideaway for the city's Ticos (a.k.a. locals) to enjoy.

She told us that with "sandias y cervezas" – watermelons and beer – we'd make fast friends. I relayed the good news to Greg, who speaks Portuguese but not Spanish, and I saw him flash a smile. I paid for our supplies and with some extra direction from the woman, we learned how to direct a taxi to the right spot along the highway.

It was almost sundown as we stepped back onto the street, so we decided to head straight to the rock baths. Greg whispered as we walked, "I wonder what other secrets that lady's hiding behind her counter."

———

"Want beer?" I asked in Spanish, holding up a few cans above the steam and passing them to our neighbors sitting in a pool of thermal water.

"This is pretty wild, dude. Who would have guessed there's a rainforest paradise hanging out behind some trees on the side of a random highway?" Greg said while slamming a watermelon on a pointed rock.

He stuck a spoon in my half of the watermelon and passed it to me. "Yeah man. It's amazing. Refreshing, too. Too bad it's so dark now. I can't even take a picture," I lamented.

"Maybe that's part of the beauty," Greg said. "I mean, we just have to enjoy it in the moment, you know? It's one of those things we'll get to remember in our heads."

I sank down and dipped my head below the water. Bubbles leaked from my nose as they escaped back to the surface. I thought about Greg's words after drowning out the sounds around me. We had completed most of our journey at this point, but I was just beginning to realize that in my quest to create an extraordinary trek – documenting each step with photos and videos and searching for one high after another – I had been trading joy in the present for thrills in the future. I cared more about recounting impressive past stories than savoring them as I lived them with a beloved friend.

I obsessed over finding new highs, and I had overlooked the wonder all around me. I breezed past the simple beauty in spending time with one of my best friends. I robbed myself of the bliss found in just looking around. I was always searching for the "next big thing."

We stumbled into an incredible memory of Costa Rican hot springs and watermelons because two people were living their ordinary, everyday lives. Had we not wandered into that store and met the woman who'd sat behind its counter for years, we'd never have discovered such a picturesque, local secret. If not for the taxi driver who'd driven the same roads for years, we may never have found the hot springs along the highway's curves.

"I think it's good not to have expectations. Just to feel what we feel and find what we find," I said to Greg after emerging from the water, sharing what I'd discovered below the surface.

"Yep, I totally agree," Greg said, laying back.

I continued, "I don't think I'm very good at slowing down. I don't really soak up what's happening around me. You know? Like, I need to look at all the good our life is so full of. I think I'm supposed to be learning that."

"I also agree with that," Greg laughed as he listened to me uncover what he'd known all along.

We sat in those baths eating watermelons and drinking beer for a good while longer, appreciating the moments for what they were instead of how they compared to our expectations. The longer we sat, the more content I felt. The longer I absorbed the conversations around me, the less interested I became in moving on to the next activity. I was no longer sitting in suspense of the trip's next step. I felt free from the weight of my mental expectations. Ultimately, I was in fact seeing more of the country after deciding to slow down.

There are two battles fought on opposite fronts that block us from noticing the natural wonder in our lives. The first and more prominent battle for me is a hyper-focus on success. I forget to slow down and squeeze the learning out of my life's current season because

I'm too focused on catching the next shiny object. I don't sit still, and I miss the small miracles of life as a result. I wake up demanding something new from the world each morning, forgetting that simply waking up is a gift.

Chasing success may get us to the pinnacle in one season of life, but it leaves us searching for something more in the next. Conquest sounds big and meaningful, but the idea that increasing accomplishment can fulfill our deepest longings is a slippery temptation with no end in sight. Personally, my demands for instant gratification and my impatience for success too often disrupt the maturity that's gained through steadily pursuing a long-term goal.

The second and opposite battle we fight is apathy. Apathy leaves us feeling drained and disinterested in watching the stories unfolding all around us. It expresses itself as indifference instead of scurrying from one high to the next. It sucks your energy. It actually requires a tremendous amount of focus and intentionality to find depth and meaning in the relationships and rhythms of our everyday lives. Rich life lessons surround us all the time, but routine and familiarity can camouflage them.

Apathy is like standing in our backyards and assuming we've already turned over all the stones and counted all the rocks, so it must be time to move on. In the process, we overlook the trees, flowers, and blossoming plants waiting for us to notice their beauty. It's like taking a Rock Climbing 101 class at your local gym and concluding that scaling Mt. Everest couldn't be too different. That box has been checked! Time to move on.

Apathy is not conscious neglect. Often, we just forget to pick our heads up from the daily grind and look around.

On my worst days, I feel like I'm fighting these two battles at once. I want the high of knowing what will happen during the next chapter of my life, but without the slow build-up and steady effort required to get there. I hurry past the plush, colorful settings and dynamic characters in chapter five, instead of expending the energy to study them. As a result, I miss my chance to start chapter six with richer context and fuller appreciation.

Now, of course, we can't know when we'll breathe our last breath, so we also can't know where exactly we are in our life stories. We may have years' worth of chapters remaining, we might not. But, we do know with certainty that all stories come to an end. In rare moments of clarity, I'm able to remind myself that making it to the end isn't the goal. We were created to enjoy our stories as the plot slowly reveals itself. We shouldn't have to skip ahead to the last page.

We weren't meant to write our own stories, you see. If we were, we'd know our lives' expiration dates and we'd have total control over the events that unfolded before then.

You'll discover this as you continue reading – we're not authors, we're just characters. Each one of us was created to play a specific role in a much larger, communal story about our world. This story's collective plot, which governs every part of our lives, was set in motion by God, our Creator, centuries ago. In what I'll call the "Big Story" of our world, God included two universal themes: the principle of paradox and the story framework. These two themes are the keys to discovering deeper meaning and greater purpose in the ordinary and everyday moments of our lives, including my life and your own (no backpacking trips required, by the way).

references

[1] Curtin, M. (2017, February 27). This 75-Year Harvard Study Found the 1 Secret to Leading a Fulfilling Life. Retrieved from https://www.inc.com/melanie-curtin/want-a-life-of-fulfillment-a-75-year-harvard-study-says-to-prioritize-this-one-t.html

[2] Bailey, M. (2014, July 18). Michael Barry: the truth about cycling domestiques. Retrieved from https://www.telegraph.co.uk/men/active/10951513/Michael-Barry-the-truth-about-cycling-domestiques.html

[3] Lewis, C. S. (2017). *Mere Christianity*. Harper Collins Publishers.

[4] Horton, A. P. (2018, November 29). The Five Types of Impostor Syndrome And How To Beat Them. Retrieved from https://www.fastcompany.com/40421352/the-five-types-of-impostor-syndrome-and-how-to-beat-them

[5] Goff, Bob. (2018). *Everybody always: becoming love in a world full of setbacks and difficult people*. Nashville, TN: Nelson Books, an imprint of Thomas Nelson.

[6] The parable of the two debtors in modern terms. (2018, April 8). Retrieved from https://chimesnewspaper.com/13189/opinions/parable-two-debtors/

[7] Bonhoeffer, D. (2015). *The Cost of Discipleship*. London: SCM Press.

[8] Bonhoeffer, D., & Staats, R. (n.d.). *Barcelona, Berlin, New York: 1928-1931; Dietrich Bonhoeffer Works* (Vol. 10). Minneapolis, MN: Fortress Press.

[9] Nagel, T. (2009). *What Does It All Mean? A Very Short Introduction to Philosophy*. New York: Oxford University Press.

[10] Doretsays, D., Waymansays, B., Ferdoussays, M. F., Lorenz, Nelsonsays, B., & Chowdhurysays, A. R. (2016, October 21). Chaos Theory and the Logistic Map. Retrieved from https://geoffboeing.com/2015/03/chaos-theory-logistic-map

[11] Lewis, C. S. (2017). *Mere Christianity*. Harper Collins Publishers.

[12] *Ibid.*

[13] *Ibid.*

[14] RTÉ One. (2015, February). *The Meaning of Life*. Stephen Fry.

[15] Lewis, C. S. (1996). *The Case for Christianity*. New York: Simon & Schuster.

[16] Kensinger, E. A. (n.d.). Negative Emotion Enhances Memory Accuracy. *Current Direction in Psychological Science*, 16(4), 213–218. Retrieved from https://www2.bc.edu/elizabeth-kensinger/Kensinger_CD07.pdf

[17] Nouwen, H. J. M. (1997). *Bread for the Journey*. San Francisco: Harper San Francisco.

[18] McGinty, J. C. (2017, February 17). Is Your Attention Span Shorter Than a Goldfish's? Retrieved from https://www.wsj.com/articles/is-your-attention-span-shorter-than-a-goldfishs-1487340000

[19] Association, P. (2014, March 7). Winter storms in England 'caused greatest loss of trees in a generation'. Retrieved from https://www.theguardian.com/environment/2014/mar/07/winter-storms-england-loss-trees

[20] "Principle 5: 'Let the Other Person Save Face.'" How to Win Friends and Influence People, by Dorothy Carnegie, Simon & Schuster, 1981.

[21] Ferdman, R. (2015, June 16). The rise of humblebragging, the best way to make people not like you. Retrieved from https://www.washingtonpost.com/news/wonk/wp/2015/06/16/the-rise-of-humblebragging-the-best-way-to-lose-your-friends-respect/

[22] Lewis, C. S. (2017). *Mere Christianity*. Harper Collins Publishers.

[23] The OEC: Facts about the language. (n.d.). Retrieved from https://web.archive.org/web/20111226085859/http:/oxforddictionaries.com/words/the-oec-facts-about-the-language

[24] Alessandretti, L., Sapiezynski, P., Sekara, V., Lehmann, S., & Baronchelli, A. (2018, June 18). Evidence for a conserved quantity in human mobility. Retrieved from https://www.nature.com/articles/s41562-018-0364-x

[25] How Americans spend their time. (n.d.). Retrieved from https://graphics.wsj.com/time-use/

[26] Stearns, P. N. (1999). *Battleground of desire: the struggle for self-control in modern America*, p. 98. New York: New York University Press.